≈ THE ≈
GIFT
OF AGE

Other Treasury Books
A Treasury for Cat Lovers
A Treasury for Dog Lovers
A Tribute to Teachers
Presidential Trivia and *American Trivia*
(with Caroline McCullagh) (forthcoming)

Also by Richard Lederer
Adventures of a Verbivore
Anguished English
The Ants Are My Friends (with Stan Kegel)
Basic Verbal Skills (with Philip Burnham)
The Bride of Anguished English
Building Bridge (with Bo Schambelan and Arnold Fisher)
The Circus of Words
Classic Literary Trivia
Cleverly Comical Animal Jokes (with Jim Ertner) (forthcoming)
Comma Sense (with John Shore)
Crazy English
The Cunning Linguist
Fractured English
Get Thee to a Punnery
The Giant Book of Animal Jokes (with Jim Ertner)
Have Yourself a Punny Little Christmas
Literary Trivia
A Man of My Words
The Miracle of Language
More Anguished English
The Play of Words
Pun & Games
Puns Spoken Here
The Revenge of Anguished English
Rip Roaring Animal Jokes (with Jim Ertner) (forthcoming)
Sleeping Dogs Don't Lay (with Richard Dowis)
Super Funny Animal Jokes (with Jim Ertner)
Wild and Wacky Animal Jokes (with Jim Ertner)
The Word Circus
Word Play Crosswords, vols. 1 and 2 (with Gayle Dean)
Word Wizard
The Write Way (with Richard Dowis)

~THE~
GIFT
OF AGE

Wit and Wisdom, Information and Inspiration
for the Chronologically Endowed,
and Those Who Will Be

RICHARD LEDERER
Illustrations by Jim McLean

Marion Street Press

Portland, Oregon

Acknowledgments

I have striven mightily to track down the source of every item in this book that isn't of my own making. To those creators whom I have not been able to identify, I hope you are pleased that your luminous contributions gleam, albeit anonymously, from these pages.

A version of "The Way We Word" appeared in *AARP The Magazine*, March/April 2005. A version of "Never Say Die" appears in my *Get Thee to a Punnery* (Gibbs Smith 2006).

Published by Marion Street Press
4207 S.E. Woodstock Blvd. # 168
Portland, Ore. 97206-6267
USA

http://www.marionstreetpress.com

Orders and review copies: 800-888-4741

Printed in the United States of America

ISBN 978-1-933338-85-9

Copyedited by Lorna Gusner

Back cover photo by Kim Treffinger

Library of Congress Cataloging-in-Publication Data

Lederer, Richard, 1938-
   The gift of age : wit and wisdom, information and inspiration for the chronologically endowed, and those who will be / Richard Lederer ; illustrations by Jim McLean.
       p. cm.
    ISBN 978-1-933338-85-9
  1. Aging--Humor. 2. Old age--Quotations, maxims, etc. I. Title.
   PN6231.A43L43 2011
   818'.5407--dc22

                                          2010026998

To my brother Milt, who shows me
how to grow old gracefully and graciously.
–*Richard Lederer*

To my parents, Slim and Lucille.
They not only gave me life,
but through precept and example,
encouraged me to live it with gusto!
–*Jim McLean*

Contents

Introduction

No spring nor summer beauty hath such grace
As I have seen in one autumnal face.
–JOHN DONNE

In the end, it's not the years in your life that count.
It's the life in your years.
–ABRAHAM LINCOLN

I'm button-burstingly proud to announce that I recently turned seventy-two years of youth.* Now that I've passed through the portal of my biblical threescore years and ten, I've reached the point in my life when I have stopped lying about my age. Rather, I brag that I am so full of years. I'm no longer a spring chicken; I'm a winter chicken. I'm no longer wet behind the ears; I'm dry behind the years. I'm no longer knee high to a grasshopper; I'm sky high above a grasshopper. I'm not a has-been; I'm an about-to-be. Yay! Yippee! Huzzah! Woo-hoo! What a ride!

Some of us try to turn back our life's odometer. Others of us want people to know why we look this way. We admit that we have bumps and dents and scratches in our finish, and the paint job is getting a little dull. And sure, the fenders are too wide to be in style, and our seats are sagging. The battery no longer holds a charge, and the headlights have dimmed. The hoses are brittle, and much

*Jim McLean, the illustrious illustrator of this book, is eighty-two.

of the original tire tread is worn away. The transmission stays in low gear and doesn't easily shift to high. Climbing any hill is liable to cause sputtering. And whenever we sneeze or cough, our radiator seems to leak.

But you know what? We've traveled many, many miles, and some of the roads weren't paved. Wisdom and laughter are our shock absorbers. We've become classics.

And we're not alone: In 2010, the year this book was completed, 518 million men and women worldwide are sixty-five or older, including one out of every eight people in the United States.

While growing older is mandatory, feeling old is optional. Attitude is ageless. More than two millennia ago, the Greek playwright Sophocles wrote: "One must wait until the evening to see how splendid the day has been." Only at sunset is the day truly golden. The later the hour of the day, the longer the shadow you cast.

Gentle Reader: You'll never be younger again than you are right now! You may be over the hill, but that's better than being under the hill—and it's not till you're going downhill that you really pick up speed! Birthdays are good for you: The more of them you have, the longer you live.

The poet Robert Browning wrote, "Grow old along with me! The best is yet to be. The last of life, for which the first was made." May *The Gift of Age* (printed in fourteen-point type) set you to laughing and learning about the best years of your life.

There is only one way to live a long life, and that is to age. And there is only one way to age—with a smile. If you are able to laugh at yourself, you'll never cease to be amused. After all, you're only old once.

Richard Lederer
San Diego, California
richard.lederer@pobox.com

Why It's Great to Be Chronologically Endowed

The great thing about getting older
is that you don't lose all the other ages you've been.
—MADELEINE L'ENGLE

One advantage of getting old.
So many people do not share my past
that I am free to invent it.
—ALFRED KAZIN

No wise man ever wished to be younger.
—JONATHAN SWIFT

Americans grow happier as they grow older, according to a recent University of Chicago study that is one of the most thorough examinations of happiness ever conducted in the United States. Starting in 1972, the researchers asked a large cross section of Americans the question "Taken all together, how would you say things are these days—would you say that you are very happy, pretty happy, or not too happy?" Consistently, older people expressed more happiness than younger ones.

In 2008, an extensive telephone survey of 340,000 Americans, ages eighteen to eighty-five, confirmed the results of the University of Chicago study. The data, published in *The Proceedings of the National Academy of*

Sciences, revealed that, on average, feelings of stress and inadequacy increase from ages eighteen to fifty, after which feelings of well being steadily take center stage. The upshot is that most people are happier in their early eighties than they are in their thirties.

Hence, dear reader, if you happen to be under fifty and feeling gloomy, look on the bright side: You have years of old age to look forward to!

As they grow older, Americans also grow wiser. A recent University of Michigan study has been called "the single best demonstration of a long-held view that wisdom increases with age." Responding to narratives of social conflict, the participants sixty and older showed a better ability to recognize others' values and points of view and to accept change and uncertainty. In other words, as we age, we accumulate social wisdom.

Yes indeed, fullness of years makes for fullness of life. For one thing, you're surrounded by a lot of friends: As soon as you wake up, Will Power is there to help you get out of bed. Then you go and visit John. When you play golf, Charley Horse shows up to be your partner. As soon as he leaves, along come Arthur Ritis and his six aunts— Aunt Acid, Auntie Pain, Auntie Oxidant, Auntie Biotic, Auntie Coagulant, and Auntie Inflammatory—and you go the rest of the day from joint to joint. After such a busy day, you're Petered and Tuckered out and glad to go to bed—with Ben Gay, of course!

And you're so cared for—eye care, dental care, long-term care, private care, intensive care, eldercare, and Medicare.

Another benefit of great maturity is that you're worth a fortune. You have silver in your hair, gold in your teeth, stones in your kidneys, lead in your feet, mineral deposits in your joints, and natural gas in your stomach.

CHAPTER 1

Here's another medical fact (and I'm not making this up): Studies show that one's body temperature declines from decade to decade and that the drop becomes particularly pronounced in the elderly. Therefore, old folks are the coolest people on earth.

But wait! There's more—many more advantages to attaining old age:

- You've reached the third age of man—youth, maturity, and "you're looking wonderful!" And you can't look wonderful for your age until you've grown old.
- Each year you experience less peer pressure.
- There is nothing left to learn the hard way.
- You can sing in the bathroom while brushing your teeth.
- You can say, "When I was your age . . ." to more and more people.
- If you are taken hostage, you will be among the first to be released.
- You can eat dinner at 4:00 PM.
- Senior discounts.
- You can brazenly spoil the grandkids and then send them back home to their parents.
- You don't have a bedtime.
- No more zits.
- No more pregnancy scares.
- No more Phys Ed, ugly gym uniforms, Algebra, diagramming sentences, pop quizzes, final exams, SATs, study halls, or detentions.
- You watch movies that you saw when you were young, and now realize that you had no idea what the heck was going on when you first saw them.
- Fewer things seem worth waiting in line for.
- The speed limit is no longer a challenge to you.

- Your joints are now more accurate than the National Weather Service.
- You no longer have to spend big bucks to get your teeth whitened.
- If you do something naughty, nobody calls your parents.
- Nobody expects you to run into a burning building.
- All those things you couldn't have as a youth you no longer want.
- Your ears and nose may be growing bigger, your skin may be wrinkling, and your nose and chin may be sprouting hair, but your failing eyesight doesn't record all those changes.
- At class reunions you feel younger than everybody else looks.
- Your investment in health insurance is finally paying off.
- Whatever you buy now won't wear out.
- Thanks to acid reflux, you *can* eat your cake and have it, too.
- You tolerate pain better than younger people because you know that pain is better than no sensation at all.
- People no longer view you as a hypochondriac.
- Any sexual harassment charges filed against you will probably be dismissed.
- You can wrap your own Christmas presents and hide your own Easter eggs.
- Adult diapers are actually kind of convenient.
- You feel righteous because memory loss passes for a clear conscience.
- The older you get, the better you were!
- It's such a nice change from being young.
- You are in possession of a gift that too many others have been denied.

2

Age Before Beauty

Beautiful young people are accidents of nature.
But beautiful old people are works of art.
–ELEANOR ROOSEVELT

Is not wisdom found among the aged?
Does not long life bring understanding?
–JOB 12:12

Years may wrinkle the skin,
but to give up enthusiasm wrinkles the soul.
–GENERAL DOUGLAS MACARTHUR

It seems as if only now I really know who I am.
My strengths, my weaknesses, my jealousies—
it's as if all of it has been boiling in a pot for all these years,
and as it boils, it evaporates into steam,
and all that's left in the pot in the end is your essence,
the stuff you started out with in the very beginning.
–KIRK DOUGLAS

Old age, I have come to see, is a gift.

As a chronologically endowed American, I am now, probably for the first time in my life, the person I have always wanted to be. I think of myself as a "sage"— "experienced," "wise," "seasoned," "venerable," and "well tempered."

Oh, not my body! I sometimes despair over my body— the wrinkles, the baggy eyes, the spots on my hands, the sagging rear. And often I am taken aback by that old person that lives in my mirror. But I don't agonize over those things for long. I know that, as the years accumulate, the beauty steals inward.

I would never trade my amazing friends, my wonderful life, and my loving family for less gray hair or a flatter belly. As I've aged, I've become more kind to myself, and less critical of myself. I've become my own friend.

I don't chide myself for eating that extra cookie, or for not making my bed, or for buying that silly ceramic gecko that I didn't need but that looks so avant-garde on my patio. I am entitled to a treat, to be messy, to be extravagant. I have seen too many dear friends leave this world too soon, before they understood the great freedom that comes with aging. Whose business is it if I choose to

16

read or play on the computer until 4 AM and sleep until noon? It is my choice to eat dessert every single day that I feel like it.

I will dance with myself to those wonderful tunes of the '40s and '50s and '60s and '70s. And if I, at the same time, wish to weep over a lost love, I will. I will walk the beach in a swimsuit that is stretched over a bulging body, and will dive into the waves with abandon if I choose to, despite the pitying glances from the firm and slim of body. Never mind them. They, too, will grow old.

I know I am sometimes forgetful, but that's in part because I have more life to remember. Then again, some memories are just as well forgotten. And I eventually remember the important things.

Sure, over the years my heart has been broken. How can your heart not break when you lose a loved one, or when a child suffers, or even when somebody's beloved pet is hit by a car? But broken hearts are what give us strength and understanding and compassion. A heart never broken is pristine and sterile and will never know the joy of being imperfect.

I am so blessed to have lived long enough to have my hair turning gray, and to have my youthful laughs forever etched into deep grooves on my face. So many have never laughed, and so many have died before their hair could turn silver. So many do not receive the gift of age.

As I get older, I find it is easier to be positive. I care less about what other people think. I don't question myself anymore. I have even earned the right to be wrong.

I like being old. It has set me free. I like the person I have become. I am not going to live forever, but while I am still here, I will not waste time lamenting what could have been or worrying about what will be. The past is history. The future is a mystery. But now—this very moment—is called "the present" because it is such a precious gift.

Distinguished But Not Extinguished

They shall bear fruit even in old age.
They shall forever be fresh and fragrant.
–PSALM 92

He who has a hundred miles to walk
should reckon ninety as half the journey.
–JAPANESE PROVERB

I am always doing that which I cannot do,
in order that I may learn how to do it.
–PABLO PICASSO

The man who works and is never bored is never old.
Work and interest in worthwhile things
are the best remedy for age.
Each day I am reborn. Each day I must begin again.
–PABLO CASALS

My heroes are the two Pablos—Picasso and Casals—who
pursued their painting and cello-playing well into their 90s;
not the corporate titans whose golden parachutes landed
them safely within gated communities for unbroken days
of golf, bridge, and sunsets seen through a martini glass.
–ROY ROWAN

When the artist Francisco Goya was eighty, he drew an ancient man propped on two sticks with a great mass of white hair and a full beard. To the portrait he added this inscription: "I am still learning."

⚬⚭⚬

Oliver Wendell Holmes Jr. was and still is generally regarded as one of the most outstanding justices in the history of the U.S. Supreme Court. He was known as the Great Dissenter because he disagreed with the other judges so much. Holmes sat on the Supreme Court until he was ninety-one. Two years later, President Franklin Roosevelt visited him and found him reading Plato. "Why?" FDR asked.

"To improve my mind," Holmes answered.

In the golden sunset of his life, financier Bernard Baruch told a reporter that he intended to learn to speak fluent Greek by the end of the year.

"Mr. Baruch?" asked the reporter. "You're ninety-five years old. Why would you want to speak Greek now?"

"It's now or never," explained Baruch.

A young reporter once asked Pablo Casals: "Mr. Casals, you are ninety-five and the greatest cellist who ever lived. Why do you still practice six hours a day?"

The renowned musician answered: "Because I think I'm making progress."

Let us now praise famous men and woman who at the age of seventy or older achieved magnificently:

- Michelangelo was carving the *Rondanini Pietà* just before he died at eighty-nine. Throughout his life he proclaimed, "I am still learning."
- Anna Mary Robertson was the classic late bloomer. When her fingers became too stiff for embroidering, she started painting in her late seventies. Under the name Grandma Moses, she had her first one-woman exhibit when she was eighty and painted some sixteen hundred works to wide acclaim before dying at age one hundred and one.
- Also at the age of eighty, Jessica Tandy won an Academy Award as Best Actress in a Leading Role for her role in *Driving Miss Daisy*.
- At eighty-two, Ruth Gordon won an Emmy as Outstanding Lead Actress in a Comedy Series for her role in *Taxi*, ten years after her Oscar for Best Actress in a Supporting Role, in *Rosemary's Baby*.
- In 2010, comic actress Betty White became, at age eighty-eight, the most chronologically gifted person

to ever host *Saturday Night Live*. Her appearance on the show garnered the best ratings in eighteen months. When asked if there was anything left in show business she still wanted to do, Betty White replied, "Robert Redford."

- When she was seventy-nine years old, Grace Hopper was elevated to Rear Admiral in the U.S. Navy, the first woman to hold that rank.

- Golda Meir became Israel's first female Prime Minister at seventy-one.

- As of the writing of this book, Elizabeth II is Queen of the United Kingdom at the age of eighty-four. Should she rule for five more years, she will surpass the reign of Queen Victoria, who sat on the throne for sixty-three years until her death at the age of eighty-two.

- Ronald Reagan became president of the United States at the age of sixty-nine, one month short of his seventieth birthday—the oldest man ever to ascend to that office. So we'll count him as seventy and note that he left the presidency one month shy of seventy-eight. In a televised presidential debate against his considerably younger opponent, Walter Mondale, Reagan quipped, "I will not make age an issue in this campaign. I am not going to exploit, for political purposes, my opponent's youth and inexperience."

- In 1962, John Glenn became the fifth man to travel in space and the first American to orbit the earth. In 1998, after serving twenty-four years in the Senate, Glenn, at age seventy-seven, lifted off for a second space flight thirty-six years after his first mission. His nine-day journey as by far the oldest ever astronaut was designed to study the effects of space flight on the elderly.

A Dozen Ageless Athletes

How old would you be if you didn't know how old you are?
–LEROY SATCHELL PAIGE

The trick is growing up without growing old.
–CASEY STENGEL

It's a mere moment in a man's life
between an All-Star Game and an Old-Timers' Game.
–VIN SCULLY

Ty Cobb's lifetime batting average is .366, seven points higher than that of anyone else. He won eleven batting titles, batting .401 at the age of thirty-five and .321 at the age of forty-one.

Long after his retirement, a newspaper reporter asked Cobb how he would do playing modern baseball. "I figure I'd bat around .280," Cobb replied.

"Only .280?" asked the reporter. "But your lifetime batting average was .366."

"Yep," replied Cobb. "But keep in mind that I'm fifty-four years old."

Seriously though, here are some athletes for the ages:

1. In the 2008 Olympic Games, Dara Torres was the oldest Olympic swimmer ever, at forty-one. She captured three silver medals.

CHAPTER 4

2. Quarterback and kicker George Blanda retired from professional football at forty-eight.

3. Martina Navratilova won the mixed doubles championship at the U.S. Open at age forty-nine.

4. Gordie Howe played professional hockey (including a stint with his two sons) from 1946 to 1980, retiring at fifty-two years old.

5. Satchel Paige pitched for the Kansas City Athletics at fifty-nine.

6. Tom Watson is by far the oldest golfer ever to lead the field in a major championship. In the 2009 British Open, Watson was the leader or co-leader each of the first three rounds and right through the seventy-first hole, finally losing in a playoff. He was fifty-nine years of age, and it had been twenty-six years since he had won a major title.

7. In 2008, sixty-year-old Saoul Mamby became the oldest boxer to compete in a professional bout. Okay, he did lose to his thirty-two-year-old opponent, but he did go ten rounds.

8. When he was sixty-four, Oscar Swahn won a gold medal for shooting in the 1912 Olympic Games.

9. Clifford Batt swam the English Channel at the age of seventy.

10. In 2008, Kenny Mink became the oldest college basketball player in the United States. He was seventy-three.

11. Yuichiro Miura climbed Mount Everest in 2003 at the age of seventy-five.

12. In 2009, Hershel McGriff became the oldest driver to compete in a NASCAR-sanctioned event. He was eighty-one.

Writing for the Ages

A truly great book should be read in youth,
again in maturity and once more in old age,
as a fine building should be seen
by morning light, at noon, and by moonlight.
–ROBERTSON DAVIES

It is of the new things that men tire—
of fashions and proposals and improvements and change.
It is the old things that startle and intoxicate.
It is the old things that are young.
–G. K. CHESTERTON

I want to be thoroughly used up when I die,
for the harder I work, the more I live. . . .
Life is no "brief candle" to me.
It is a sort of splendid torch
which I have got hold of for the moment;
and I want to make it burn as brightly as possible
before handing it on to future generations.
–GEORGE BERNARD SHAW

Here, with whitened hair, desires failing,
strength ebbing out of him, with the sun gone down
and with only the serenity
and the calm warning of the evening star left to him,
he drank to Life, to all it had been,
to what it was, to what it would be. Hurrah!
–SEAN O'CASEY

When he was eighty-nine years of age, the Greek tragedian Sophocles (496–406 B.C.) was brought before a court of law by his son, who sought to have the playwright certified as suffering from senility. In his defense, Sophocles stood before his judges and read passages from *Oedipus at Colonus,* which he had lately written but not yet staged. The court dismissed the case.

This piece of literary history demonstrates that many writers who have reached a certain age have produced impressive works of literature. At age eighty, former *Washington Post* publisher Katherine Graham won a Pulitzer for her best-selling autobiography, her first and only book. Johann Wolfgang von Goethe completed his immortal *Faust* when he was eighty-three. Helen Hooven Santmyer was eighty-eight and resided in a retirement home when she gave the world *And Ladies of the Club.* Sarah and Bessie Delany wrote their first book, *Having Our Say: The Delany Sisters' First One Hundred Years* when they were one-hundred-and-three and one-hundred-and-one respectively. Four years later, in 1997, Sarah published *On My Own at 107: Reflections on a Life Without Bessie.*

A life of hard labor that began at the age of eight deprived George Dawson of an education for ninety years. He never learned to read until one day a recruiter for a local adult-literacy program knocked on the door of Dawson's home in Dallas. "I figured if I could lay a railroad tie as well as any man and cook as well as any woman, I could learn to read as well as anyone else," said Dawson. He overcame his initial reluctance to reveal his illiteracy, telling himself, "All your life you've wanted to read. Maybe this is why you're still around."

George Dawson learned not only to read; at age ninety-nine he wrote his life story in *Life Is So Good.* He'd come to know the Scriptures years earlier, but, wrote Dawson, "Now I think about God smiling when He hears me read."

He died at one-hundred-and-three, the year that he earned his GED.

These golden literary accomplishments illuminate one of the happy aspects of language in general. As our experiences with language and life deepen with age, we can become more skillful and sensitive in working with matters verbal.

But like any skill, our languaging benefits from use and practice. Just as we can add muscle to our bodies even when we're in our nineties, our brains grow stronger with aerobics of the mind and pushups of the brain. So get out there and exercise your verbal muscles. Solve a crossword puzzle. Read a book. Keep a journal. Join a writers' group. Give a talk. Try out for a play. You'll almost certainly lead a richer and longer life.

Senior Best Sellers

Here are a dozen American authors, fifty years of age or above, whose novels have become annual best sellers during the past fifty years. Match each author in the left-hand column with each book in the right-hand column.

Each number in the left-hand column signifies the author's age during the year or years (signified in the right-hand column) when their novel or novels swept America.

---

1. Jean M. Auel (54)

2. James Clavell (57)

3. Elia Kazan (58)

4. Jerry B. Jenkins (52)

5. Tim LaHaye (75)

6. Robert Ludlum (52)

7. James A. Michener (58–73)

8. Katherine Anne Porter (72)

9. Alexandra Ripley (57)

10. Irving Stone (58)

11. Leon Uris (52)

12. Robert J. Waller (53)

a. *The Agony and the Ecstasy* (1961)

b. *The Arrangement: A Novel* (1967)

c. *The Bridges of Madison County* (1992)

d. *Desecration* (2001)

e. *The Matarese Circle* (1979)

f. *Noble House* (1981)

g. *The Plains of Passage* (1990)

h. *Scarlett* (1991)

i. *Ship of Fools* (1962)

j. *The Source* (1965), *Centennial* (1974), *Chesapeake* (1978), *The Covenant* (1980)

k. *Trinity* (1976)

Answers
1. g 2. f 3. b 4–5. d 6. e 7. j 8. i 9. h 10. a 11. k 12. c

6

Signs That You're Growing Old

My dad's pants kept creeping up on him.
By sixty-five he was just a pair of pants and a head.
–JEFF ALTMAN

You know you're getting old
when you stoop to tie your shoelaces
and wonder what else you can do
while you're down there.
–GEORGE BURNS

You know you're growing older when you find
that you truly enjoy the Disney Channel specials
featuring ancient rock stars of the past
who look "hey—pretty good!"
–CATHY CRIMMINS

You know you're getting older
if you have more fingers than real teeth.
–RODNEY DANGERFIELD

You know you're getting old; there are certain signs.
I walked past a cemetery,
and two guys ran after me with shovels.
–RODNEY DANGERFIELD

Middle age is when you're sitting at home on Saturday night
and the telephone rings and you hope it isn't for you.
–OGDEN NASH

Middle age is when you've met so many people
that every new person
you meet reminds you of someone else.
–OGDEN NASH

Middle age is when your classmates are so gray
and wrinkled and bald they don't recognize you.
–BENNETT CERF

Years ago we discovered the exact point,
the dead center of middle age.
It occurs when you are too young to take up golf
and too old to rush to the net.
–FRANKLIN P. ADAMS

Middle age is when
your age starts to show around your middle.
–BOB HOPE

You know you're getting old
when the candles cost more than the cake.
–BOB HOPE

Old is the time of life
when even your birthday suit needs pressing.
–BOB HOPE

You know you're getting old
when your liver spots start to show through your gloves.
–PHYLLIS DILLER

There are many other signs that you may be more than halfway up the stairway to Heaven. Take clothing:

You have three sizes of clothes in your closet, and two of them you will never wear again.

Walmart and Target seem to share your fashion sense. You realize that all those geeky people in Bermuda shorts walking around Disney World include you. It's a documented fact that as your age climbs, so do your pants. Soon you'll have to cut eyeholes in the crotch.

As a public service, you have agreed to never appear on the beach in a Speedo again.

Even your footwear gives you away: You resort to slip-on shoes or Velcro straps. And you wear dark socks with your sandals.

You know you're growing old when ...

- The word *spry* actually applies to you.
- When people tell you that you look "great," they add "for your age."
- You still have the old spark, but it takes more puffing to ignite.
- You still have something on the ball, but you're too tired to bounce it.

- You finally reach the top of the ladder, only to find that it's leaning against the wrong wall.
- You know all the answers, but nobody asks you the questions.
- You've lived long enough to know your way around, but you're not going anywhere.
- Your favorite part of the newspaper is "Fifty Years Ago Today."
- You remember when the cost of going to a movie was less than the cost of a stamp today.
- On the golf course you try to shoot your age, but you shoot your weight instead.
- You choose your cereal for the fiber, not the toy.
- You regret that you resisted all those temptations.
- You just can't stand people who are intolerant.
- A fortune-teller offers to read your face.
- Your children are starting to wrinkle.
- Your grandkids look like they should be in middle school, yet here you are attending their college graduation.
- You subscribe to cable television for the Weather Channel.
- You have more hair on your ears than on your head.
- Your wife tells you to pull in your stomach, and you already have.
- By the time you've lit the last candle on the birthday cake, the first one has burned out.
- When you finally get all your birthday candles lit, they set off the smoke alarm.
- Your broad mind and narrow waist have exchanged places. You're 16 around the neck, 42 around the waist, and 102 around the golf course.
- You are starting to like accordion music.

- You are starting to look like the photograph on your driver's license.

- You remember old radio shows better than the TV show you watched last week. And, by the way, the radio shows were better.

- You instruct your barber never to trim hair off the top of your head.

- For your birthday you receive your first nose-hair clippers.

- You've come to the annoying realization that your parents were right about almost everything.

- You don't care where your spouse goes, just as long as you don't have to go along.

- The bus driver starts calling you *ma'am,* instead of *hey, lady.*

- It's the doctor, not the police officer, who tells you to slow down.

- If you're driving a car, it qualifies for classic plates.

- Your grandkids drive cars while you ride a bike.

- Your new La-Z-Boy has more options than your Cadillac.

- Your high school yearbook is now home to three different species of mold.

- You buy "age-defying" makeup and "anti-wrinkle" creams and believe they work.

- You turn out the lights for economic reasons instead of romantic ones.

- You have started using words like *young pup, snot-nosed kid, wet behind the ears, sonny, young lady,* and *whippersnapper.*

- You recognize Led Zeppelin songs that have been turned into elevator muzak.

- When you watch black-and-white films, you point to the screen and say, "He's dead. She's dead. They're dead."
- You've had three opportunities to buy every single Disney animated classic "for the last time in a generation."
- Your childhood toys turn up in antique stores with huge price tags on them.
- You often try to change TV channels with your cordless phone.
- You'd pay good money to be strip-searched.
- Your hair starts turning from gray to black.
- You're wearing more gold in your mouth than on the rest of your body.
- Going braless pulls all the wrinkles out of your face.
- You take your thirteen-year-old granddaughter to an amusement park, and her ticket costs more than yours.
- You have a party, and the neighbors don't even realize it.
- When you stand in front of a mirror, you can see your rear end without turning around.
- You're sitting on a park bench, and a Boy Scout comes along and offers to help you cross your legs.
- Chicken wings or cold pizza no longer qualify as day starters. You actually eat breakfast food at breakfast time.
- People send you this list (and you forget who they are).

7

The Way We Word

When you finally go back to your old hometown,
you find it wasn't the old home you missed
but your childhood.
–SAM EWING

Back in the olden days, we had a lot of moxie. We'd put on our best bib and tucker and straighten up and fly right. Hubba-hubba! We'd cut a rug in some juke joint, and then go necking and petting and smooching and spooning and billing and cooing and pitch woo in (depending on when we were making all that whoopee) flivvers, tin lizzies, roadsters, hot rods, and jalopies in some passion pit or lovers' lane. Heavens to Betsy! Gee whillikers! Jumpin' Jehoshaphat! Holy moley! We were in like Flynn and living the life of Riley, and even a regular guy couldn't accuse us of being a knucklehead, a nincompoop, or a pill. Not for all the tea in China!

Back in the olden days, life was a real gas, a doozy, a dilly, and a pip; flipsville, endsville, the bee's knees, the cat's whiskers, the cat's meow, and the cat's pajamas; far-out, nifty, neat, groovy, ducky, beautiful, fabulous, super, terrif, sweet, and copacetic. Life used to be swell, but when's the last time anything was swell? *Swell* has gone the way of beehives, pageboys, and the D.A., of spats, knickers, fedoras, poodle skirts, saddle shoes, and pedal pushers. Oh, my aching back. Kilroy was here, but he isn't anymore.

Like Washington Irving's Rip Van Winkle and Kurt Vonnegut's Billy Pilgrim, we have become unstuck in time. We wake up from what surely has been just a short nap, and before we can say, *Bob's your uncle!* or *I'll be a monkey's uncle!* or *This is a fine kettle of fish!* we discover that the words we grew up with, the words that seemed omnipresent as oxygen, have vanished with scarcely a notice from our tongues and our pens and our keyboards. Poof, poof, poof go the words of our youth, the words we've left behind. We blink, and they're gone, evanesced from the landscape and wordscape of our perception, like Mickey Mouse wristwatches, Hula-hoops, skate keys, candy cigarettes, little wax bottles of colored sugar water, and an organ-grinder's monkey.

Where have all those phrases gone? Long time passing. Where have all those phrases gone? Long time ago. *Pshaw. The milkman did it. Think about the starving Armenians. Bigger than a bread box. Banned in Boston. The very idea! It's your nickel. Don't forget to pull the chain. Knee high to a grasshopper. Turn-of-the-century. Iron curtain. Domino theory. Fail-safe. Civil defense. Fiddlesticks! You look like the wreck of the Hesperus. Cooties. Going like sixty. I'll see you in the funny papers. Don't take any wooden nickels. Heavens to Murgatroyd! And awa-a-ay we go!*

Oh, my stars and garters! It turns out there are more of these lost words and expressions than Carter had liver pills.

The world spins faster, and the speed of technical advance can make us dizzy. It wasn't that long ago that, in the course of a typical lifetime, only the cast of characters playing out the human drama changed. Now it seems the text of the play itself is revised every day.

Hail and farewell to rumble seats, running boards, and crank-down car windows. Iceboxes and Frigidaires. Victrolas and hi-fi's. Fountain pens and inkwells. Party lines. Tennis presses (and "rough and smooth" and white tennis balls in metal cans that you opened with a key). Slide rules. Manual typewriters. Corrasable Bond. Ditto for Photostats and mimeographs. (Do you, like me, remember that turpentiney smell of the mimeo fluid?)

The inexorable advance of technology shapes our culture and the language that reflects it. We used to watch the tube, but televisions aren't made of tubes anymore, so that figure of speech has disappeared. We used to dial telephone numbers and dial up people and places. Now that almost all of us have converted from rotary to push-button phones, we search for a new verb—"Sorry, I must have pushed the wrong number"; "I think I'll punch up Doris"; "I've got to index-finger the Internal Revenue Service"; *Press M for Murder* and watch *dial* dying on the vine. With modern radios, can the demise of "don't touch that dial!" be far behind?

How many more years do *hot off the press, hung out to dry, put through the wringer,* and *carbon copy* have, now that we no longer print with hot lead, hang wet clothes on clotheslines, operate wringer washing machines, and copy with carbon? Do any young folks still say, *This is where we came in*? The statement means the action or situation is starting to repeat itself, and it comes from the movies. Today there are so many ways of finding out exactly when a movie begins, but back in the olden days we'd get to the theater at pretty much any time and walk in at random. We might watch the last half of a movie and then some (no longer shown in multiplexes) trailers, a newsreel, cartoons, and a serial that always ended at the most harrowing moment so that you just *had* to come back next week—and then the second movie in the double feature, and then the beginning of the first movie, until the point where we could say, *This is where we came in.*

Do I sound like a broken record? Do you think I must have been vaccinated with a phonograph needle? In our high-tech times, these metaphors fade away, like sepia photographs in a family album.

Technology has altered our sense of the size of the world and the things in it. Remember the thrill your family felt owning that six-inch black-and-white rabbit-eared television set (soon to be known as the *boob tube* and *idiot box*)?

Today more and more TV screens are upwards of forty inches. We drive bigger cars, live in bigger homes, eat bigger meals, and inhabit bigger bodies. I am 6'3" and I used to be called a *six-footer*. Now the NBA is studded with at least a dozen *seven*-footers, and outstanding female athletes, such as Lisa Leslie, Maria Sharapova, and Venus Williams, majestically top six feet, so *six-footer* has lost its magic.

How to respond to the supersizing of America? That's the $64 question. The $64 question was the highest award in the 1940s radio quiz show *Take It or Leave It*. By the 1950s, inflation had set in, and $64 no longer seemed wondrous. Then in 1955 came *The $64,000 Question*. The popularity of the show helped *the $64,000 question* become a metaphor for a question whose answer could solve all our problems, but the expression has faded from our lives because that once sumptuous figure no longer impresses us. Neither does *millionaire* command our awe anymore, now that there are more than two million millionaires in the United States.

While our bodies and our possessions have expanded, our world has grown smaller, and the language of distance has changed. Remember that admonition *Shhh. I'm on long distance!*? Phrases like *long distance* and *coast to coast* and even *worldwide* used to hold such excitement for us. Now we take them for granted, so we hardly ever use them.

During the past century, the English language has added an average of nine hundred to a thousand new words a year. As freshly minted words have enriched the currency of our language, the meanings of the words we grew up with have changed under our eyes and ears. A *hunk* no longer means simply a large lump of something, and *rap* isn't just '60s talk. *Crack* means more than just a small opening, *ice* more than frozen water, and *pot* more than a cooking utensil. A *pocket* isn't just for pants, and a *bar code* is no longer ethics for lawyers or the etiquette of behavior in a café. A *pound* is no longer just a unit of currency or measurement but that tipsy tic-tac-toe game that sits above the *3* on your keyboard or below the *9* on your telephone.

Remember when *IBM* was something a two-year-old might say to a parent? The computer, the most deeply striking technology of our lifetimes, has powerfully challenged our sense of so many hitherto uncomplicated words: *back up, bit, boot, cookie, crash, disk, flag, hacker, icon, mail, memory, menu, mouse, pop-up, scroll, spam, viral, virus,* and *window.*

This can be disturbing stuff, this winking out of the words of our youth, these words that lodge in our heart's deep core. But just as one never steps into the same river twice, one cannot step into the same language twice. Even as one enters, words are swept downstream into the past, forever making a different river. We of a certain age have been blessed to live in changeful times. For a child, each new word is like a shiny toy, a toy that has no age. We at the other end of the chronological and language arc have the advantage of remembering there are words that once did not exist, and there were words that once strutted their hour upon the earthly stage and now are heard no more, except in our collective memory. It's one of the greatest advantages of aging. We can have archaic and eat it too.

8

Remember When

When you're forty, half of you belongs to the past—
and when you're seventy, nearly all of you.
–JEAN ANOUILH

Nothing is more responsible for the good old days
than a bad memory.
–FRANKLIN P. ADAMS

The older a man gets, the further
he had to walk to school as a boy.
–JOSH BILLINGS

Can you remember when all electrical gadgets worked with simply a single "on" and "off" switch?

Can you remember when you would drive into a gas station and get your windshield cleaned, oil checked, and gas pumped for free without asking? And you didn't pay for air for your tires, and you got trading stamps to boot?

Can you remember when the family would gather around the kitchen table to read the Sunday comics—*The Katzenjammer Kids, Dick Tracy, Mutt and Jeff, Bringing Up Father* (with Jiggs and Maggie), and *Li'l Abner* (with shmoos)?

Can you remember when the family would gather around the radio to listen to FDR's fireside chats; *The Shadow; Jack Armstrong, All-American Boy; The Fred Allen Show;*

Allen Show; Fibber McGee and Molly; Amos and Andy; The Breakfast Club; Captain Midnight; and *Buck Rogers?* Ah, those radio commercials: "I'm Buster Brown. I live in a shoe. That's my dog Tige. He lives there, too." "More bounce to the ounce," and "Call for Philip Morris!"

Or when the family would gather around the six-inch black-and-white TV set (a Philco, Admiral, or Motorola that took forever to warm up) to watch *Arthur Godfrey and His Friends, Howdy Doody, Leave It to Beaver, Ozzie and Harriet, Beanie and Cecil, Your Show of Shows, Your Hit Parade, I Love Lucy, My Three Sons,* the original *Twilight Zone,* and "Uncle Milty" on *Texaco Star Theater?*

Those were the days of test patterns; rabbit ears on the TV set; outdoor antennas; television stations that went off at midnight when the National Anthem played; and the white dot on the screen that became smaller and smaller when you turned off your television set. Because remote controls

40

did not exist, we actually had to get up and walk to the TV to turn it on and off, and to change channels and volume. And that television was the only one in the home.

Those were the days when we watched TV in a dark room, with the big magnifier clamped to the TV screen, sometimes with blue, pink, and green bands running across to add color to the sky, the people, and the grass. While we watched, we ate TV dinners placed on TV trays. And, of course: *Shhhh. No talking* while watching television! Talking would be as impolite as yakking in a movie theater.

Do you remember? Do you remember? Then, dearie, you're as old as I.

- *Red rover, red rover; olly olly oxen free; double-dog dare; eenie-meenie-miney-moe; one potato, two potato, three potato, four; red light, green light! Simon says, "Take one giant step"; Mother, may I?*
- drive-in movies
- Burma Shave signs
- coffee shops with tableside jukeboxes
- fast-food restaurants whose waiters and waitresses would clamp a tray to your driver's side window and bring you (sometimes on roller skates) your meal
- Studebakers (you couldn't tell if they were coming or going), Plymouths, Mercurys, Packards, Nashes, DeSotos, LaSalles, Hudsons, and Essexes
- Marathon and Powerhouse bars, Turkish Taffy, Kern's Butterscotch, and Chicken Dinner candy
- Blackjack, Clove, and Teaberry chewing gum
- deposits on soft drink bottles (which were all made of glass)
- the holes in the caps of the Royal Crown Cola bottles so that Mother could sprinkle the clothing before ironing

- home milk delivery in glass bottles, with cardboard stoppers (and the separators to remove the cream first)
- iceboxes, blocks of ice, and the sound of the ice pick chipping away
- grandfather clocks
- flypaper
- corsets and girdles
- telephone numbers with a word prefix (mine was Allegheny-5491)
- blackboards that were always black
- cash registers (with their distinctive ping)
- Keds and P. F. Flyers
- hand push lawnmowers
- human pinsetters at bowling alleys
- Kools, Old Golds, Chesterfields, and lots of cigarette and pipe smokers
- Butch Wax (for your flat top)
- zoot suits
- the 98-lb. weakling getting sand kicked in his face
- turntables and 78 rpm records
- S&H Green Stamps pasted in booklets to redeem merchandise
- the Fuller Brush man
- door-to-door encyclopedia salesmen
- a single red light atop police cars
- hi-fis
- wax lips and wax panpipes
- trash cans of burning leaves in the back yard or set next to the curb
- rug beaters
- metal ice cube trays, with levers
- Brownie cameras and blue flash bulbs

- coal bins
- noisy typing classes
- cherry bombs
- Indian burns
- Dixie cups attached by long pieces of tight string that became a short-distance telephone
- five-cent packs of baseball cards
- leg painting during the rationing in World War II so that women looked as if they were wearing nylon stockings

If you remember most of these items, you are indeed chronologically endowed.

9

Valued Memories

Before my mother would give you that dime allowance,
she'd want you to do a little chore around the house,
like build a porch.
–RAY ROMANO

Super seniors are sometimes asked, "What was your favorite fast food growing up?"

They answer, "We didn't have fast food when we were growing up. All the food was slow."

"C'mon, seriously. Where did you eat?"

"It was a place called home, and a woman called Mom cooked for each dinner and canned for the winter. When Dad got home from work, we all sat down together around the dining room table. If I didn't like what Mom put on my plate, I was allowed to sit there until I did like it. If I wished to leave the table, I had to get permission."

Not only are you, gentle reader, chronologically endowed. You are values-endowed, for you lived at a time when "family values" ruled. Those were the days, my friend. We thought they'd never end. Days when . . .

• At home, Mom was always there for you.

• A babysitter was called a mother.

• A shoemaker stuck to his last, and husbands and wives stuck to their first.

- Families sat down to dinner to count their blessings, not their calories.
- A dishwasher wasn't something that could be purchased.
- Children who misbehaved to get attention got it. Child guidance was something parents were expected to administer, not submit to.
- Male teachers wore neckties, and female teachers wore high heels and had their hair done frequently.
- In school, we memorized The Gettysburg Address, long poems, and passages from Shakespeare.
- No lipsticks were kissproof, but most girls were.
- In the movies, the hero and heroine didn't kiss until the end. There were no movie ratings. They weren't needed.
- Charity was a virtue, not an organization.
- Air was clean, and sex was dirty.
- Unmentionables were also unseeables.
- Dirty words in books were dots and dashes.
- We didn't have to buy what we couldn't afford.
- We didn't start shopping for Christmas until after Thanksgiving.
- Nobody owned a purebred dog.
- A garage housed a car, not a boat and a bunch of junk.
- People actually sent handwritten letters to each other.
- T-shirts were clothing, not billboards for advertisements.
- People who wore blue jeans worked.
- A job was the first thing we went steady with.
- A day's work took only a day.
- A service charge included service.

- A great many boys delivered newspapers seven days a week, rising at 6:00 AM. It cost seven cents a newspaper, and the paperboy got to keep two cents. On Saturday, the paperboy would collect forty-two cents from each customer. His favorite customers were the ones who gave him fifty cents and told him to keep the change. His least favorites were the ones who never seemed to be home on collection day.

- Doctors made house calls, and everything needed to cure you they brought along in a little black bag.

- Back then, we would reach into a muddy gutter for a penny—and a quarter was a pretty good allowance.

- People who came to pick you up rang the doorbell, rather than blowing the horn.

- No one ever asked where the car keys were because they were always in the car's ignition, and the doors were never locked.

- When a teenager went into a garage, he came out with a lawnmower.

- It was considered a privilege to be taken out to dinner at a real restaurant with our parents.

- The worst thing we thought we could catch from the opposite sex was cooties.

- We played baseball and two-hand-touch football with no adults to help us with the rules of the game.

- Little League had tryouts, and not everyone made the team. Those who didn't had to learn to deal with disappointment.

- Some students weren't as smart as others, so they failed a grade and were held back to repeat the same grade.

- Test scores were not adjusted for any reason.

- Just about the scariest thing that could happen to us was the principal calling our parents.

- The idea of a parent bailing us out if we broke a law was unheard of. Our parents actually sided with the law. Our actions were our own—and there were consequences.

- In speaking and writing, we were taught to put others before us and ourselves last, as in "My mother, my sister, and I went to the grocery store." These days it's "me first!" as in "Me and Taylor went shopping." When they next revive the famous Rodgers and Hammerstein musical, it'll be re-titled *Me and the King*!

- We fell out of trees, got cut, and broke bones and teeth, but there were no lawsuits from these events. They were simply accidents. No one was to blame but us.

Libraries Changed Our Lives

A Library implies an act of faith
Which generations still in darkness hid
Sign in their night in witness of the dawn.
–VICTOR HUGO

Elinor Lander Horwitz once wrote in *The Washington Post:* "There are numerous men and women perambulating the earth—in appearance much like ordinary respectable citizens—who have warm, loving, passionate, even sensuous feelings about libraries." After I (your user-friendly author) published a column tracing the history of libraries in the United States, Gertrude King Ramstrom, of Nashua, New Hampshire, sent me her "warm, loving, passionate, even sensuous feelings" about her childhood adventures in a New England library. Her testimonial makes vivid William Shakespeare's claim that "my library was dukedom large enough."

Dear Sir: Your article about libraries whisked me back in time and place to the 1920s and the little village of Haydenville, Massachusetts, where I grew up. Its tiny library, which is still in use, was our only avenue of adventure to the wonders of the outside world, and my brothers and I, along with our friends, made good use of it.

It is not a very imposing building either in architecture or size, and a traveler probably would not even realize one was there. Although it is on Main Street, it is tucked back at an angle to the road and has a mien of withdrawal, or shyness, as if aware of its insignificance among the libraries of the world. But to us it was a structure of great importance.

Its single room is shaped like the letter *H* with the crosspiece widened to include almost the entire area. Wonderful little nooks, furnished with stools and chairs, are formed by the extensions of the vertical bars of the *H*, and that was where we acquired a glimpse of the world, had our curiosity aroused, and met with our friends. It was open every Friday evening, and directly after supper Mother made us wash up and comb our hair so we would look respectable and be clean enough to inspect books without leaving fingerprints. Most of our friends were doing the same, and about 7:00 PM we congregated on the wide stone step of the building.

On summer evenings we lingered outside to talk, but in winter it was nice to push into the room and stand over the one-pipe register and allow the heat to blow up around us. There were no rules about talking, except when we became too boisterous, so the boys jostled and joked in one nook while we girls squeezed into another to whisper and giggle.

In our little library was born my love of history, which became my major in college. From *The Colonial Twins, The Puritan Twins,* and *The Twins of the American Revolution* through *The Red Badge of Courage* and *With Malice Toward None,* I read, and am still reading, every historical novel available. By corroborating their assertions with the facts of history, I have found a never-ending source of enlightenment.

While my brothers read *The Bobbsey Twins, Tom Swift,* and *Huck Finn*, I read *Pollyanna, Bambi,* and

The Yearling. As we grew, my older brother turned to *Twenty Thousand Leagues Under the Sea* and almost wore out Lindberg's *We.* I can still picture the blue binding of the book with a silver airplane etched on the cover and my brother slouched in a big easy chair with his leg dangling over its arm. Both socks wrinkled around his ankles showing bare legs below the cuffs of his knicker pants, and his hand rumpled his hair as he soared high over the earth with his hero.

As he traveled the skies and seas, I traversed America with Willa Cather, learned to love animals through Albert Payson Terhune stories, found goodness in life with A. J. Cronin, and whisked away on the whimsy of Elizabeth Goudge. It was a wonderful experience, and because of it I would add another beatitude to the ones we learned back in our Sunday School days: Blessed are they who can read and enjoy a good book for theirs is the world and its kingdoms.

I firmly believe that children are influenced by what they read and that the books we took home from the library impressed upon us what Mother and Dad tried to teach—that good character and high moral values are to be desired above all other attributes. We heard it, we read it, and so we lived it. There is no greater endowment that can be given a child than an ideal and a hero, and our little library did just that for us.

11

Why We Should Be Dead

The essence of childhood, of course, is play,
which my friends and I did endlessly
on streets that we reluctantly shared with traffic.
–BILL COSBY

When I was a kid, we had a quicksand box.
I was an only child, eventually.
–STEVEN WRIGHT

I could tell that my parents hated me.
My bath toys were a toaster and a radio.
–RODNEY DANGERFIELD

Safety was not a big thing when I was growing up.
A seat belt was something that got in the way.
"Ma, the seat belt is digging into my back."
"Stuff it down into the seat. And roll those windows up.
You're letting my cigarette smoke out."
–MARGARET SMITH

Do you remember when nobody used sunscreen and many of us used baby oil, iodine, and silver sun reflectors to intensify the rays of the sun on our faces?

Do you remember the fluoroscopes in shoe stores? These machines turned our feet green, showed our foot bones, and allowed us to see how well new shoes would fit us by shooting X-rays into our feet.

Do you remember playing with matches and running with scissors?

According to today's medical experts, those of us who were kids before the 1970s probably should not have survived:

- As infants, we were put to sleep on our tummies in baby cribs covered with bright-colored, lead-based paints.

- As children, we would ride in cars with no car seats, booster seats, seat belts, or air bags. We had no childproof lids on bottles of pills and medicines and no childproof latches on doors, cabinets, or electric outlets.

- When a thermometer broke, we would play with the mercury and roll little mercury balls into one big mercury ball.

- We rode out diphtheria, measles, scarlet fever, and whooping cough.

- Hardly anybody got tested for allergies.

- We survived being born to mothers who smoked and drank, took aspirin, and ate blue cheese dressing and tuna from a can while they were pregnant.

- Our mothers used to cut chicken, chop eggs, and spread mayo on the same cutting board with the same knife and no bleach, and we'd eat hamburger raw off that board.

- Our homes were filled with pipes wrapped in asbestos.

- Our bicycles weighed fifty pounds and had one speed: slow. When we rode our bikes, we wore baseball caps, not helmets. Many bikes didn't have chain guards, and even though we wore pant-leg clips, sometimes our pants got caught in the bicycle chains.

CHAPTER 11

- We fired slingshots, peashooters, popguns, cap pistols, and BB guns at each other.
- We ate cupcakes and bread and butter and drank heavily sugared soda pop, but we were never overweight because we were always outside playing.
- We actually hitchhiked.
- We rode in the back of pickup trucks with no benches or seat belts.
- We drank water from the garden hose and not from a bottle.
- We shared one soft drink from one bottle with four friends, and no one died from this.
- Atomic warfare was an everyday threat. We actually thought that "duck and cover"—hiding under a desk away from a window and closing our eyes tightly—could protect us against radioactive explosions.
- We spent hours building our go-carts out of scraps and then tore down the hill, only to find out we forgot the brakes.
- We left home in the morning and played all day, as long as we were back when the streetlights came on.

- Cell phones did not exist. No one was able to reach us all day.
- We didn't have Playstations, Nintendo 64s, XBoxes, video games, three hundred channels on cable, DVD movies, surround sound, personal computers, Internet chat rooms, or texting. We should have been bored to death.
- But we had friends! We went outside and found them.
- We rode bikes or walked to a friend's home and knocked on the door or rang the bell or just walked in and talked to them.
- We punched each other hard and got black and blue and learned to get over it.
- We made up games with sticks and tennis balls and ate worms, and although we were warned, we didn't put out very many eyes, nor did the worms live inside us forever.
- We played dodgeball, and sometimes the ball would really hurt.
- In playgrounds on hot summer days, we slid our scrawny butts down scalding sliding boards perched on steaming asphalt.
- We showed off our vaccination scars.
- We were never given Novocain or laughing gas in the dentist's chair.
- We set off fireworks on the Fourth of July without police supervision.
- And, alas, there was polio. Our parents were frantic that we avoid contracting this infantile paralysis. So, especially in the summer, they kept us away from crowds, parks, and swimming pools. Remember iron lungs, the March of Dimes, and—glory be—Albert Sabin and Jonas Salk.

Somehow we survived. We endured and prevailed.

The Lighter Side of Aging

Humor keeps the elderly rolling along, singing a song.
When you laugh, it's an involuntary explosion of the lungs.
The lungs need to replenish themselves with oxygen.
So you laugh, you breathe, the blood runs,
and everything is circulating.
If you don't laugh, you'll die.
–MEL BROOKS

Wrinkles should merely indicate where smiles have been.
–MARK TWAIN

We humans possess six senses—sight, hearing, smell, taste, touch—and our sense of humor. We don't stop laughing because we grow old; we grow old because we stop laughing. Hey, the only thing seniors can crack without hurting themselves is a joke:

A Senior Prayer

Grant me the senility to forget the people I never liked anyway, the good fortune to run into the ones I do, and the eyesight to tell the difference.

Virus Alert!

Warning! Please beware and be wary of an unstoppable virus. This bug targets people born before 1960, and even the most advanced programs, from Norton to McAfee, seem unable to protect this part of our population.

As a public service, here are the symptoms of this dreaded affliction:

1. You hit "Send" before you mean to send. As a result, some of the e-mails you send are blank or incomplete.
2. You send e-mails to the wrong people.
3. You send multiple copies of the same e-mail.
4. You send e-mails to the people who sent them to you before you have typed a reply.
5. You forget to attach attachments.
6. When typing in e-mail addresses, you constantly confuse *.com, .net, .org,* and *.edu.*
7. You mistakenly empty your "Deleted Items" file.
8. You hit "Delete" when you mean to hit "Send."
9. Even worse, you hit "Send" when you mean to hit "Delete."
10. You can't remember if you've already sent someone a message. ("Oh oh, have I sent you this message before?")

If you demonstrate some of these symptoms, you are a victim of the "C-Nile Virus."

Checklist

One holiday season, a mother decided that she was no longer going to remind her children of their thank-you note duties. As a result, they never acknowledged the generous checks they'd received from their grandmother.

The next year, things were different. All the grandchildren came to see the grandmother and thank her profusely for her generosity.

What caused the change of behavior? This time, grandma hadn't signed the checks.

A Real-Life Newspaper Headline

CHICAGO CHECKING ON ELDERLY IN HEAT

A Real-Life Newspaper Correction

Due to a telephonic error in transmission, we stated yesterday that Mr. Max Steinberg will be knighted next month. In fact, he will be ninety next month.

Department Chairs

Two old men, one a retired professor of psychology and the other a retired professor of history, were sitting around on the porch of a retirement home, watching the sun set. The professor of history said to the professor of psychology, "Have you read Marx?"

To which the professor of psychology replied, "Yes, I think it's the wicker chairs."

Burning the Candle

A woman walked up to a little old man rocking in a chair on his porch. "I couldn't help noticing how happy you look," she said. "What's your secret for such a long happy life?"

"I smoke three packs of cigarettes a day," he said. "I also drink a case of whiskey a week, eat fatty foods, never exercise, and chase women whenever I can."

"That's amazing," the woman said. "How old are you?"

"Twenty-six."

Heaven . . . I'm in Heaven

An eighty-eight-year-old couple had been married for more than sixty years when they both died in a car crash. They had been in excellent health right up to the end, mainly due to her interest in health food and exercise.

When they reached the pearly gates, St. Peter took them to their mansion, which was decked out with a beautiful kitchen and master bath suite with Jacuzzi and surrounded by magnificent landscaping. As they oohed and aahed, the old man asked Peter how much all this was going to cost.

"It's free," Peter replied. "This is Heaven."

Next they went out back to survey the championship golf course that the home backed up to. They would have golfing privileges every day, and each week the course changed to a new one representing the great golf courses back on earth.

The old man asked, "What are the greens fees?"

Peter answered, "This is Heaven. You play for free here."

Then they went to the clubhouse and saw the lavish buffet lunch with the great cuisines of the world laid out.

"How much will it cost to eat?" asked the old man.

"This is Heaven. It's free!" Peter replied benevolently.

"Well, where are the low-fat and low-cholesterol tables?" the old man asked timidly.

Peter explained, "That's the best part. You can eat as much as you like of whatever you like and you never get fat and you never get sick. This is Heaven."

With that the old man went into a fit of anger, slamming down his hat, stomping on it and shrieking. Peter and the man's wife both tried to calm him down and asked him what was wrong. The old man looked at his wife and said, "This is all your fault. If it weren't for your blasted health food diets, we could have been here ten years ago!"

Goodbye, Mr. Chips

An elderly man lay dying in his bed. Although at death's door, he smelled the aroma of his favorite chocolate chip cookies wafting up the stairs. He gathered his remaining strength and lifted himself from the bed. Leaning against the wall, he slowly made his way out of the bedroom and, with even greater effort, forced himself down the stairs, gripping the railing with both hands. With labored breath, he leaned against the doorframe and gazed into the kitchen.

Were it not for the intense pain he was feeling, he would have thought himself already in Heaven. There, spread out on the kitchen table and counters, were trays of his favorite chocolate chip cookies.

Was it Heaven? Or was it one final act of love from his devoted wife, seeing to it that he departed this world a happy man? Mustering one final, heroic effort, he lurched toward the table, landing on his knees. His cracked lips parted, and the wondrous cookie taste was already in his mouth, seemingly bringing him back to life.

"Stay away from those cookies," warned his wife. "They're for the funeral."

A Sub Par Performance

An avid eighty-year-old golfer moved to a new town, joined the local country club, and asked to play a match with the pro. The pro said he would play with him and asked how many strokes he wanted for a bet. The old man answered, "I really don't need any strokes because I'm an experienced player. The only real problem I have is getting out of sand traps."

Even though it was his first time on the course, the octogenarian shot a steady par. Coming to the par-four eighteenth, the old guy and the pro were all even. The pro made a nice drive and was able to get on the green and two-putt for par. The old gentleman made a nice drive, too, but his approach shot landed in a sand trap next to the green.

Playing from the bunker, he hit a high ball that landed on the green and rolled into the hole! Birdie, match, and all the money!

The pro walked over to the sand trap where his opponent was still standing. "Nice shot," complimented the pro, "but I thought you said you have a problem getting out of sand traps?"

Replied the octogenarian, "I do. Please give me a hand."

Gene Rations

In the examining room, a doctor said to his patient, "You're in great shape for a sixty-year-old."

"Who says I'm sixty?" replied the patient. "I'm eighty."

"That's remarkable! So how old was your father when he died?"

"Who says he's dead? He'll be a hundred and three this year."

"Wow! You have a great family history. How old was your grandfather when he died?"

"Who says he's dead? My grandfather just turned one hundred and twenty-five, and he's getting married next month."

"Incredible! But at his age why would he ever want to get married?"

"Who says he wants to?"

The Art of the Comeback

My son has a new nickname for me: "Baldy."
Son, I've got a new word for you: "Heredity."
–DAN SAVAGE

Is Chivalry Dead?

An elderly lady entered a room, and an elderly gentleman sitting there did not stand up for her. "I see that you're not so gallant as when you were a boy," the lady huffed.

"And I see that you're not so buoyant as when you were a gal," the man riposted.

A Tactful Development

Photographer Ruth Van Bergen specialized in celebrity portraits. One wealthy woman complained that Van Bergen's photo wasn't nearly as good as the first one she had taken a decade ago.

"You simply must forgive me, my dear," the diplomatic photographer said. "The last time I took your picture, I was ten years younger."

A Put-down of Biblical Proportions

Dorothy Parker once arrived at a narrow doorway at the same time as Clare Booth Luce. "Age before beauty," said Mrs. Luce, stepping aside.

"Pearls before swine," said Mrs. Parker, gliding through.

Making Sense of Aging

On the TV show *Hollywood Squares*, the question was asked, "Which of your five senses tends to diminish as you get older?"

Charlie Weaver answered, "My sense of decency."

HOLLYWOOD SQUARES

Looking Ahead

Three elderly gentlemen were talking about what their grandchildren would be saying about them fifty years in the future.

"Fifty years from now, I would like my grandchildren to say, 'He was successful in business,'" declared the first man.

CHAPTER 13

"Fifty years from now," said the second, "I want them to say, 'He was a loyal and loving family man.'"

The third senior explained, "Fifty years from now, I want them all to say, 'He certainly looks good for his age!'"

Inventive Invective

A self-important college freshman took it upon himself to explain to a senior citizen sitting next to him why it was impossible for the older generation to understand his generation.

"You grew up in a different world, actually almost a primitive one," he said, in a voice loud enough for many nearby to hear. "We, the young people of today, grew up with television, jet planes, space travel, and men walking on the moon. Our spaceships have visited Mars, we have nuclear energy, electric and hydrogen cars, computers with light-speed processing, and . . ." He paused to take another swig of beer.

The senior citizen took advantage of the pause to say, "You know, son, you're right. We didn't have those things when we were young, so we *invented* them. Now, you arrogant little twit, what are *you* doing for the next generation?"

The applause from those sitting near the two was deafening.

Humorists on Aging

- I used to be quite an athlete myself . . . big chest, hard stomach, but all that's behind me now.–*Bob Hope*

- I don't feel old. In fact, I don't feel anything until noon. Then it's time for my nap.–*Bob Hope*
- After seventy, you still chase women, but only downhill. –*Bob Hope*
- Youth is wonderful. It's a shame to waste it on the young.–*Mark Twain*
- You can't reach old age by another man's road. My habits protect my life, but they would assassinate you. –*Mark Twain*
- Age is strictly a case of mind over matter. If you don't mind, it doesn't matter.–*Jack Benny*
- Except for an occasional heart attack, I feel as young as I ever did.–*Robert Benchley*
- Last night I had a typical cholesterol-free dinner: baked squash, skimmed milk, and gelatin. I'm sure this will not make me live any longer, but I know it's going to seem longer.–*Groucho Marx*
- Age is not a particularly interesting subject. Anyone can get old. All you have to do is live long enough. –*Groucho Marx*
- A man is only as old as the woman he feels. –*Groucho Marx*
- I care about our young people, and I wish them great success, because they are our Hope for the Future, and someday, when my generation retires, they will have to pay us trillions of dollars in social security.–*Dave Barry*
- I recently had my annual physical examination, which I get once every seven years, and when the nurse weighed me, I was shocked to discover how much stronger the Earth's gravitational pull has become since 1990.–*Dave Barry*
- Some sad news: The world's oldest man has died in Japan at 114. What's the deal with this world's oldest

title? It's like some kind of curse, have you noticed. As soon as you get it, like, a year later you're dead. –*Jay Leno*

- I stay away from natural foods. At my age I need all the preservatives I can get.–*George Burns*

- People are always asking me when I'm going to retire. Why should I? I've got it two ways—I'm still making movies, and I'm a senior citizen, so I can see myself at half price.–*George Burns*

- If you live to be one hundred, you've got it made. Very few people die past that age.–*George Burns*

- We could certainly slow the aging process down if it had to work its way through Congress.–*Will Rogers*

- I'm at an age where food has taken the place of sex in my life. In fact, I've just had a mirror put over my kitchen table.–*Rodney Dangerfield*

- Inflation is when you pay fifteen dollars for the ten-dollar haircut you used to get for five dollars when you had hair.–*Sam Ewing*

- I don't plan to grow old gracefully. I plan to have face-lifts until my ears meet.–*Rita Rudner*

- At age eighty-two, I sometimes feel like a twenty-year-old, but there's seldom one around.–*Milton Berle*

- Always be nice to your children because they are the ones who will choose your rest home.–*Phyllis Diller*

- I don't know how you feel about old age, but in my case I didn't even see it coming. It hit me from the rear.–*Phyllis Diller*

- By the time a man is wise enough to watch his step, he's too old to go anywhere.–*Billy Crystal*

- I know I'm getting older. I pulled my left shoulder out putting peanut butter on a bagel. It was chunky, though. I pulled out my right shoulder putting Ben Gay on my left shoulder.–*Jeff Cesario*

- Looking fifty is great—if you're sixty.–*Joan Rivers*
- Talk about getting old. I was getting dressed and a Peeping Tom looked in the window, took a look, and pulled down the shade.–*Joan Rivers*
- You can live to be a hundred if you give up all the things that make you want to live to be a hundred. –*Woody Allen*
- Like everyone else who makes the mistake of getting older, I begin each day with coffee and obituaries. –*Bill Cosby*
- I recently turned fifty, which is young for a tree, mid-life for an elephant, and ancient for a quarter miler whose son now says, "Dad, I can't run the quarter with you anymore unless I bring something to read." –*Bill Cosby*
- The secret of staying young is to live honestly, eat slowly, and lie about your age.–*Lucille Ball*
- The elderly don't drive that badly. They're just the only ones with time to do the speed limit.–*Jason Love*
- To get back my youth I would do anything in the world, except take exercise, get up early, or be respectable. –*Oscar Wilde*
- All my life, I always wanted to be somebody. Now I see that I should have been more specific.–*Lily Tomlin*
- Don't go to a school reunion. There'll be a lot of old people there claiming to be your classmates.–*Tom Dreesen*
- Don't worry about avoiding temptation. As you grow older, it will avoid you.–*Joey Adams*
- When I was in Boy Scouts, I slipped on the ice and hurt my ankle. A little old lady had to help me cross the street.–*Stephen Wright*
- Oldness is highly relative. The more relatives you have, the faster you age.–*Eric Nicol*

- I have discovered the secret formula for a carefree Old Age: IYCRI = FI—"If You Can't Recall It, Forget It." –*Goodman Ace*
- It used to be that my age and waist size were the same. Unfortunately, they still are.–*Reno Goodale*
- The state of Israel just turned sixty-two. It won't be long before it moves to Florida.–*Amy Poehler*
- Do you realize that the only time in our lives when we like to get old is when we're kids? You're so excited about aging that you think in fractions. You're never "thirty-six-and-a-half," but you're "four-and-a-half, going on five!" You become twenty-one, you turn thirty, you're pushing forty, you reach fifty, you make it to sixty, you build up so much speed you hit seventy. Then a strange thing happens. If you make it over a hundred, you become a little kid again. "I'm a hundred-and-one, and a half!"–*Larry Miller*
- There's one more terrifying fact about old people: I'm going to be one soon.–*P. J. O'Rourke*
- Life begins at forty—but so do fallen arches, rheumatism, faulty eyesight, and the tendency to tell a story to the same person three or four times.–*William Feather*
- My mother is going to have to stop lying about her age because pretty soon I'm going to be older than she is.–*Tripp Evans*
- Age does not diminish the extreme disappointment of having a scoop of ice cream fall from the cone. –*Jim Fiebig*
- In a survey for *Modern Maturity* magazine, men over seventy-five said they had sex once a week. Which proves that old guys lie about sex too.–*Irv Gilman*
- People are living longer than ever before, a phenomenon undoubtedly made necessary by the thirty-year mortgage.–*Doug Larson*

- I was thinking about how people seem to read the Bible a whole lot more as they get older. Then it dawned on me—they're cramming for their final exam.–*George Carlin*

- Few things are more satisfying than seeing your children have teenagers of their own.–*Doug Larson*

- My grandmother was a very tough woman. She buried three husbands, and two of them were just napping. –*Rita Rudner*

- My parents are in their sixties, but they're still having sex. They want grandchildren.–*Wendy Liebman*

- The reason grandparents and grandchildren get along so well is that they have a common enemy. –*Sam Levinson*

Grandkids Say the Darnedest Things

If nothing is going well, call your grandmother.
–ITALIAN PROVERB

Grandchildren are loving reminders
of what we're really here for.
–JANET LANESE

Grandmas are just antique little girls.
–G. W. CURTIS

If becoming a grandmother was only a matter of choice,
I should advise every one of you straightaway to become one.
There is no fun for old people like it.
–HANNAH WHITEHALL SMITH

Few things are more delightful
than grandchildren fighting over your lap.
–DOUG LARSON

I've learned that when your newly born grandchild
holds your little finger in his little fist,
you're hooked for life.
–ANDY ROONEY

*The closest friends I have made all through life
have been people who also grew up close
to a loved and loving grandmother or grandfather.*
–MARGARET MEAD

*If I'd known grandchildren
were going to be so much fun,
I'd have had them first.*
–ERMA BOMBECK

Why are grandparents like a piece of string? They're handy to have around and easily wrapped around the fingers of their grandchildren.

A third-grade girl wrote this kid's-eye view of grandparents:

A grandmother is a lady who has no children of her own. She likes other people's little girls. A grandfather is a man grandmother. He goes for walks with the boys and they talk about fishing and tractors and like that. Grandmothers don't have anything to do except be there. They're old so they shouldn't play hard or run. It is enough if they drive us to the market where pretend horses are and have lots of dimes. Or if they take us for a walk, they should slow down past things like pretty leaves or caterpillars.

Usually they are fat but not too fat to tie your shoes. They wear glasses and funny underwear. They can take their teeth and gums off. When they read to us, they don't skip or mind if it is the same story again.

It is better if they don't typewrite or play cards except with us. They don't have to be smart, only answer questions like "Why do dogs hate cats?" and "How come God isn't married?"

Everybody should try to have a grandmother, especially if you don't have television, because grandmothers are the only grownups who have got time.

The Whole Tooth

While working for an organization that delivers lunches to elderly shut-ins, a mother took her four-year-old daughter on the afternoon rounds. The little girl was unfailingly intrigued by the various appliances of old age, particularly the canes, walkers, and wheelchairs. One day the mother found her daughter staring at a pair of false teeth soaking in a glass. Eyes wide as saucers, the girl turned and whispered, "The tooth fairy will never believe this!"

The Good Old Days

A grandmother was telling her little granddaughter what her own childhood was like: "We used to skate outside on a pond. I had a swing made from a tire; it hung from a tree in our front yard. We rode our pony. We picked wild raspberries in the woods."

Taking all this in, the wide-eyed little girl said, "I sure wish I'd gotten to know you sooner!"

A Good Idea

A grandmother was playing with her little grandson. The boy's older sister exclaimed, "Grandma, you sure like to play with little kids. You should have children of your own one day!"

The Arkives

Staring at his grandfather, a five-year-old asked, "Grandpa, were you on the ark when the Flood came?"

"No, certainly not."

"Well, then, why weren't you drowned?"

Turning Over an Old Leaf

A grandmother was showing her little grandson the old family Bible. As the boy was turning the yellowed pages, a pressed tree leaf fell out. Wide-eyed, he exclaimed, "Gosh, this must be where Adam and Eve left their clothes!"

Passing with Flying Colors

Grandma didn't know if her granddaughter had learned her colors yet, so she decided to test the little girl. Grandma pointed to something and asked what color it was. Granddaughter answered correctly each time, but Grandma was having so much fun with the game that she continued with it.

After more time passed, the little girl said sagely, "Grandma, I think you should try to figure out some of these yourself!"

Starting from Scratch
A boy called his grandfather to wish him a happy birthday. When the boy asked how old he was, Grandpa told him, "seventy-two." The grandson was quiet for a moment, and then he asked, "Did you start at one?"

OMG
A little boy asked his grandmother, "Grandma, do you know how you and God are alike?"

Grandma mentally polished her halo as she asked, "No, how are we alike?"

"You're both old."

Doing a Number on Grandpa
When a little boy asked his grandfather how old he was, Grandfather teasingly replied, "I'm not sure."

"Look in your underwear, Grandpa," the boy advised. "Mine says I'm four to six."

It Doesn't Compute
Six-year-old Leonard was playing a game on his computer. He asked his grandfather what kind of games he played on his computer when he was a boy. "Back then we didn't have computers," Grandpa explained.

Leonard looked puzzled, "But how did you get your e-mail?"

Youthful Curiosity
One day a little girl was sitting and watching her mother do the dishes at the kitchen sink. She suddenly noticed that her mother had several strands of white hair sticking out in contrast to her brunette hair.

She looked at her mother and inquisitively asked, "Why are some of your hairs white, Mom?"

Her mother replied, "Well, every time that you do something wrong and make me cry or unhappy, one of my hairs turns white."

The little girl thought about this revelation for a while and then asked, "Momma, how come all of grandma's hairs are white?"

The Plane Truth

When the bus stopped to pick up young Chris for preschool, the driver noticed an older woman hugging him as he left his home. "Is that your grandmother?" the driver asked.

"Yes," said Chris. "She's come to visit us for Christmas."

"How nice," the driver said. "Where does she live?"

"At the airport," Chris replied. "Whenever we want her, we just go there and get her."

Practice Makes Perfect

A little girl was perched on her grandfather's lap as he read her a bedtime story. From time to time, she would take her eyes off the book and reach up to touch his wrinkled cheek. Then she asked, "Grandpa, did God make you?"

"Yes, sweetheart," he answered. "God made me a long time ago."

"Oh," the little girl paused. "Grandpa, did God make me, too?"

"Yes, indeed, honey," he said. "God made you just a little while ago."

"God's getting better at it, isn't He?"

A Senior's Garden
of Light Verse

I still have two abiding passions.
One is my model railway, the other—women.
But at the age of eighty-nine,
I find I am getting just a little too old for model railways.
–PIERRE MONTEUX

The Wise Old Owl

A wise old owl sat in an oak.
The more he saw, the less he spoke.
The less he spoke, the more he heard.
Why can't we be like that wise old bird?

The Eyes Have It

My face in the mirror isn't wrinkled or drawn.
My house isn't dirty. The cobwebs are gone.
My garden looks lovely, and so does my lawn.
I think I might never put glasses back on.

The Shape We're In

There's nothing whatever the matter with me;
I'm just as healthy as I can be.
I have arthritis in both of my knees;
And when I talk, I talk with a wheeze.
My pulse is weak, and my blood is thin,
But I'm awfully well for the shape I'm in.

Arch supports I have for my feet,
Or I wouldn't be able to walk on the street.
Sleep is denied me night after night,
And every morning I look a sight.
My memory's failing. My head's in a spin.
But I'm awfully well for the shape I'm in.

The moral is, as this tale we unfold,
That for you and me who are growing old,
It is better to say, "I'm fine," with a grin,
Than to let them know the shape we're in.

A Piller of Society

A row of bottles on the shelf.
Makes me analyze myself.
One yellow pill I have to pop
Goes to my heart so it won't stop.

A little white one that I take
Goes to my hands so they won't shake.
The blue ones that I use a lot
Tell me I'm happy when I'm not.

The purple pill goes to my brain
And tells me that I have no pain.
The capsules tell me not to wheeze
Or cough or choke or even sneeze.

The red one, smallest of them all,
Goes to my blood so I won't fall.
The orange ones, so big and bright,
Prevent my leg cramps in the night.

Such an array of brilliant pills
Helping to cure all kinds of ills—
But what I'd really like to know
Is what tells each one where to go?

Pondering Old Age

How do I know that my youth is all spent?
Well, my get-up-and-go has got up and went.
But in spite of it all I am able to grin
When I recall where my get-up has been.

Old age is golden, so I've heard it said;
But sometimes I wonder when I get into bed,
With my ears in a drawer and my teeth in a cup,
My eyes on the table until I wake up.

Before sleep dims my eyes, I say to myself,
"Is there anything else I should lay on the shelf?"
And I'm happy to say as I close my door,
My friends are the same, perhaps even more.

When I was young, my slippers were red,
I could kick up my heels right over my head.
When I grew older, my slippers were blue,
But still I could dance the whole night through.

Now I am old, and my slippers are black.
I walk to the store and puff my way back.
The reason I know my youth is all spent:
My get-up-and-go has got up and went.

But I really don't mind when I think, with a grin,
Of all the grand places my get-up has been.
Since I have retired from life's competition,
I busy myself with complete repetition.

I get up each morning, and dust off my wits,
Pick up my paper and read the obits.
If my name isn't there, I know I'm not dead,
So I eat a good breakfast and go back to bed.

Today's Grandmother

In the dim and distant past,
When life's tempo wasn't so fast,
Grandma used to rock and knit,
Crochet, tat, and babysit.

When the kids were in a jam,
They could always call on Gram.
But today she's in the gym,
Exercising to keep slim.

She checks the Web and surfs the Net,
Sends some e-mail, makes a bet.
Nothing seems to stop or block her,
Now that Grandma's off her rocker.

You Are Old, Father William

"You are old, Father William," the young man said,
"And your hair has become very white;
And yet you incessantly stand on your head—
Do you think, at your age, it is right?"

"In my youth," Father William replied to his son,
"I feared it might injure the brain;
But now that I'm perfectly sure I have none,
Why, I do it again and again."

"You are old," said the youth, "as I mentioned before,
And you've grown most uncommonly fat;
Yet you turned a back-somersault in at the door—
Pray, what is the reason of that?"

"In my youth," said the sage, as he shook his gray locks,
"I kept all my limbs very supple
By the use of this ointment—one shilling a box—
Allow me to sell you a couple?"

"You are old," said the youth, "and your jaws are too weak
For anything tougher than suet,
Yet you finished the goose, with the bones and the beak—
Pray, how did you manage to do it?"

"In my youth," said his father, "I took to the law,
And argued each case with my wife;
And the muscular strength which it gave to my jaw
Has lasted the rest of my life."

"You are old," said the youth. "One would hardly suppose
That your eyes are as steady as ever;
Yet you balanced an eel on the end of your nose—
What has made you so awfully clever?"

"I have answered three questions, and that is enough,"
Said his father. "Don't give yourself airs!
Do you think I can listen all day to such stuff?
Be off, or I'll kick you downstairs!"

                                        –*Lewis Carroll*

17

Great Expectations—for Life

I want to die young at an advanced age.
–MAX LERNER

The rapid progress true science now makes
occasions my regretting sometimes that I was born so soon.
It is impossible to imagine the height to which may be carried
the power of man over matter.
All diseases may be by sure means prevented or cured,
not excepting that of even old age,
and our lives lengthened at pleasure.
–BENJAMIN FRANKLIN

A young man photographing Winston Churchill on his eightieth birthday remarked, "I hope I can do the same on your hundredth birthday."

"I don't see why not," rejoined the Prime Minster. "You look reasonably fit to me."

We're living longer and better than ever before in the saga of humankind. Currently, the fastest growing segment of the population is eighty-five-year-olds and above. Here are the average life expectancies in years for human beings throughout history:

- Cro-Magnons: 25
- Ancient Greeks: 28
- Europeans in the Middle Ages: 31.3

CHAPTER 17

- Americans in 1900: 47.3
- Americans today: 78
- Americans today who have reached 65: 83.4

Our Long-Lived Presidents

On average, presidents of the United States live a long time. John Adams, born in 1735, lived to ninety years and eight months, longer than any other chief executive until Ronald Reagan, who died at ninety-three years and four months. Two years later, Gerald Ford died at ninety-three years and five months, a record that will likely be broken again and again.

Although the average life span of Americans born in the eighteenth century was less than forty years, our first ten presidents lived an average of 77.6 years:

1. George Washington: 67   6. John Quincy Adams: 80
2. John Adams: 90   7. Andrew Jackson: 78
3. Thomas Jefferson: 83   8. Martin Van Buren: 79
4. James Madison: 85   9. William Henry Harrison: 68
5. James Monroe: 73   10. John Tyler: 71

10 Tips for Living a Long Time

Centenarians are the country's fastest growing age group, having more than doubled since 1990. According to the U.S. Census Bureau, in 2000, there were 50,454 centenarians in the United States, one per 5,578 people, or roughly eighteen per 100,000. Between 2010 and 2060 the percentage in the number of American centenarians is estimated to grow 660%—to more than 300,000. The largest number of centenarians live in California and New York, while South Dakota and Iowa boast the highest proportion of residents one hundred years or older.

In 2008, one hundred centenarians were polled by telephone. Here are their top ten tips for healthy aging—along with the percentage of how many said the tip is "very important." Each centenarian polled could call more than one tip "very important."

1. Stay close to your family and friends: 90%
2. Keep your mind active: 89%
3. Laugh and have a sense of humor: 88%
4. Stay in touch with your spirituality: 84%
5. Continue looking forward to each new day: 83%
6. Keep moving and exercising: 82%
7. Maintain a sense of independence: 81%
8. Eat right: 80%
9. Keep up with news and current events: 63%
10. Keep making new friends: 63%

A Late-Edition Dictionary

Age, n. That period of life in which we compound for the vices that we still cherish by reviling those that we have no longer the enterprise to commit.
–AMBROSE BIERCE

One could define *old age* as that time of life when . . .

- Actions creak louder than words.
- Everything hurts, and what doesn't hurt doesn't work.
- Winking at a girl is closing one eye to reality.
- You're grounded for several days after flying high for one night.
- You want to see how long your car will last instead of how fast it will go.
- You should be mending your weighs.

Here's a start on a dictionary for seniors:

aging. A supposed ripening into wisdom that we nonetheless try to delay as long as possible.

all-nighter. Not having to get up to use the bathroom.

birthday. The key to longevity. The more you have, the longer you've lived.

birthday candles. A way of making light of age.

centenarian. Someone a hundred years old or more who never smoked, or who smoked all her life. He drank whiskey for eighty years, or he never used the stuff. She was a vegetarian, or she was a dedicated carnivore. He exercised vigorously every day, or he was a complete couch potato. Follow these rules carefully and you too can be a centenarian.

childhood. The time in life when you make funny faces in the mirror, in contrast to old age, the time in life when the mirror gets even.

consciousness. That annoying time between naps.

crow's feet. What other people have. On you, they're laugh lines.

dandruff. Chips off the old block.

death. A breath-taking experience.

elderberry. 1. The oldest fruit. 2. An old gravedigger.

elderhostel. Your anger as a senior when you are stereotyped as helpless.

experience. 1. What you acquire just after you needed it. 2. The name you give to your mistakes. 3. What enables you to recognize a mistake when you make it again.

Florida. God's waiting room.

funerals. Reunions for seniors.

getting a little action. You don't need to take a laxative.

getting lucky. You find your car in the parking lot.

the good old days. What people will be calling the present time fifty years from now.

grandchildren. 1. The brightest human beings on earth, even if their father (your son-in-law) is an idiot. 2. The only people who can get more out of you than the IRS. 3. Those who are driven crazy by the same person who drove you crazy.

grandparents. 1. A grandchild's press agents. 2. The most inexpensive, enduring, and simplest toy of all—one that even the youngest child can operate with ease. 3. The people who think their grandchildren are wonderful even though they're sure their children are not raising their children right. 4. An old man and old lady who keep their grandchildren's parents from spanking them.

hair. A head covering you either lose, or that migrates to your ears and nose.

happy hour. A nap.

impotence. Emission impossible.

irrepressible. Hopelessly wrinkled.

laxative. 1. What makes you a regular guy and keeps you on the go. 2. An aid to arriving at a solution by a process of elimination.

liquidity. When you look at the value of your retirement fund and wet your pants.

a night out. Sitting on the patio.

old person. 1. Anyone fifteen years older than you are. 2. One who will do anything to feel better except give up what's been making her feel bad. 3. One who is losing his hair, his teeth, and his illusions.

organ recital. Talking about your maladies.

retirement. 1. The day when you return from work and say, "Hi, honey, I'm home forever!" 2. Life's longest coffee break. 3. Doing nothing without the fear of getting caught. 4. A time in life when you switch bosses, from the one who hired you to the one who married you. 5. A time of no pressure, no stress, and no heartache, unless you play golf. 6. When there's never enough time to do all the nothing you want. 7. When you leave the rat race and learn to live on less cheese.

time. A great healer but a lousy beautician.

tying one on. Fastening your MedicAlert bracelet.

weightlifting. Trying to stand up from a sitting position.

wrinkle. 1. The nick of time. 2. Yesterday's dimple. 3. What other people have. On you it's a character line.

19

New Lists for Olden Goldies

You're never too old to become younger.
–MAE WEST

The Five Ages of a Man

1. He believes in Santa Claus.
2. He doesn't believe in Santa Claus.
3. He dresses up to look like Santa Claus.
4. He looks like Santa Claus.
5. He thinks he's Santa Claus.

Senior Stats

- **518 million**. Current population of people age sixty-five and older in the world.
- **974 million**. The total worldwide senior population over age sixty-five by 2030, projected by the U.S. Census Bureau.
- **86.7 million**. Projected number of people in the U.S. who will be sixty-five or older in the year 2050.
- **21%**. The projected percentage that seniors will make up of the world population in 2050.
- **147%**. The projected percentage that the population sixty-five and over will increase between 2000 and 2050.
- **49%**. The projected increase in U.S. population as a whole during the same period.

Age Is Just a Number

- **60.** The age at which young people believe old age begins.
- **74.** The age at which people sixty-five and older believe old age begins.
- **60%.** The percentage of people sixty-five and older who feel younger than their age.
- **3%.** The percentage of people sixty-five and older who feel older than their age.

A Senior's Day

- Eating: **5%**
- In the bathroom: **10%**
- Sleeping: **35%**
- Looking for things you had a minute ago: **50%**

10 Tips for Senior Sex

1. Wear your glasses. Make sure your partner is actually in the bed.
2. Set your timer for three minutes, in case you doze off in the middle.
3. Set the mood with lighting. Turn them all off. That's because the most effective method of birth control for seniors is nudity.
4. Put 911 on speed dial before you begin.
5. Write partner's name on your hand, in case you forget it.
6. Keep the PoliGrip close by so that your teeth don't end up under the bed.
7. Have Tylenol ready in case you actually complete the act.
8. You may end up making love several times in a given night because you will forget about the previous times that night.
9. Make all the noise you want. The neighbors are deaf, too.
10. If you are successful, call everyone you know with the news.

CHAPTER 19

Barbie for Our Generation

In 2009, Barbie, the most popular doll in the history of toydom, turned fifty. So, at long last, we have a line of Barbies we seniors can relate to. Here are some new—and more realistic—Barbie dolls to coincide with her and our aging gracefully:

- **Bifocals Barbie**. Comes with her own set of blended lens fashion frames in six wild colors (half-frames too), neck chain, and large-print editions of *Vogue* and *Martha Stewart Living*.
- **Hot-Flash Barbie**. Press Barbie's belly button and watch her face turn beet red while tiny drops of perspiration appear on her forehead. Comes with handheld fan and tiny tissues.

- **Facial-Hair Barbie**. As Barbie's hormone levels shift, see her whiskers grow. Available with teensy tweezers and magnifying mirror.

- **Flabby-Arms Barbie**. Hide Barbie's droopy triceps with these new roomier sleeved gowns. Good news on the tummy front, too—muumuus with tummy-support panels included.

- **Bunion Barbie**. Years of disco dancing in stiletto heels have definitely taken their toll on Barbie's dainty arched feet. Soothe her sores with the pumice stone and plasters, then slip on soft terry mules.

- **No-More-Wrinkles Barbie**. Erase those pesky crow's feet and lip lines with a tube of Skin Sparkle-Spackle from Barbie's own line of exclusive age-blasting cosmetics.

- **Divorced Barbie**. Sells for $199.99. Comes with Ken's house, Ken's car, Ken's boat, and Ken's retirement fund.

Golden Oldies

You make me feel so young.
You make me feel there are songs to be sung.
And even when I'm old and gray,
I'm gonna feel the way I do today
'Cause you make me feel so young.
–JOSEF MYROW AND MACK GORDON

Think about it. In thirty years, we're going to have millions of old people walking around with tattoos and body piercings. And grunge and rap music will be their golden classics.

We who are seniors today have enjoyed popular music from the Big Band-Aid era to Slipped Disco to Hip Replacement Hop. Recently, artists of the 1960s have revised their hits with new lyrics to better appeal to aging baby boomers:

1. Herman's Hermits: "Mrs. Brown, You've Got a Lovely Walker"
2. Ringo Starr: "I Get By With a Little Help From Depends"
3. The Bee Gees: "How Can You Mend a Broken Hip?"
4. Bobby Darin: "Splish, Splash, I Was Havin' a Flash"
5. Roberta Flack: "The First Time Ever I Forgot Your Face"
6. Johnny Nash: "I Can't See Clearly Now"
7. Paul Simon: "Fifty Ways to Lose Your Liver"

8. Lionel Richie: "Once, Twice, Three Times to the Bathroom"
9. Procol Harem: "A Whiter Shade of Hair"
10. Leo Sayer: "You Make Me Feel Like Napping"
11. James Brown: "Papa's Got a Brand New Catheter Bag"
12. Abba: "Denture Queen"
13. Tony Orlando: "Knock Three Times on the Ceiling If You Hear Me Fall"
14. Helen Reddy: "I Am Woman, Hear Me Snore"
15. Leslie Gore: "It's My Procedure, And I'll Cry If I Want To"
16. Willie Nelson: "On the Commode Again"

10 Hymns for the Chronologically Endowed

Some famous hymns have been revised to suit an aging population:

1. "Give Me That Old Timers' Religion"
2. "Rock of Aging"
3. "Just A Slower Walk With Thee"
4. "It Is Well With My Soul, But My Knees Hurt"
5. "Nobody Knows The Trouble I Have Seeing"
6. "Precious Lord, Take My Hand And Help Me Up"
7. "Count Your Many Birthdays, Count Them One By One"
8. "Go Tell It On A Mountain, But Speak Up"
9. "Blessed Insurance"
10. "Guide Me, O Thou Great Jehovah, I've Forgotten Where I've Parked the Car"

21

Metaphors for Aging

All the world's a stage,
And all the men and women merely players.
They have their exits and their entrances;
And one man in his time plays many parts,
His acts being seven ages.
–WILLIAM SHAKESPEARE, *AS YOU LIKE IT*

Four hundred years after Shakespeare quilled these lines, actor Dustin Hoffman said, "If life is a three-act play, I am chronologically in my third act, but I am in the first act of my life in terms of the feeling I now have for my own worth, my talent, my gift."

Both the Bard and Hoffman have employed theater metaphors to express their insights into what they have learned about the great adventure of living. A metaphor (the word in Greek originally meant "carry beyond") is a figurative comparison of two objects or ideas that are different from each other but turn out to be alike in a significant way. Here are fifteen such comparisons that illuminate the later stages of our journey through life:

1. Getting old is like visiting an all-you-can-eat buffet. What should be hot is cold; what should be firm is limp; and the buns are bigger than anything else on the menu. –*Sammy Shore*

2. Life is like a roll of toilet paper. The closer you get to the end, the faster it goes.–*Author Unknown*

3. Time sneaks up on you like a windshield on a bug.–*John Lithgow*

4. Experience is a comb that life gives you after you've lost your hair.–*Judith Stern*

5. Gray hair is God's graffiti.–*Bill Cosby*

6. Tennis is a game for young people. Until age twenty-five, you can play singles. From there until age thirty-five, you should play doubles. I won't tell you my age, but when I played, there were twenty-eight people on the court–just on my side of the net.–*George Burns*

7. By the time a person gets to greener pastures, he can't climb the fence.–*Frank Dickson*

8. To me, life is like the back nine in golf. Sometimes you play better on the back nine. You may not be stronger, but hopefully you're wiser. And if you keep most of your marbles intact, you can add a note of wisdom to the coming generation.–*Clint Eastwood*

9. Life is like a bicycle. You don't fall off until you stop pedaling.–*Claude Pepper*

10. The older I get, the greater power I seem to have to help the world. I am like a snowball–the farther I am rolled, the more I gain.–*Susan B. Anthony*

11. Old age is like climbing a mountain. You climb from ledge to ledge. The higher you get, the more breathless you become, but your views become more extensive.–*Ingmar Bergman*

12. At my age, getting a second doctor's opinion is like switching slot machines.–*Jimmy Carter*

13. You can't turn back the clock. But you can wind it up again.–*Bonnie Prudden*

14. There are people who are beautiful in dilapidation, like old houses that were hideous when new.–*Logan Piersall Smith*

15. How beautifully leaves grow old. How full of light and color are their last days.–*John Burroughs*

Antique Bumper Snickers

Old Is In.

All Power to Old People.

Hail, Geezer!

I'm an Oldie, and I'm a Goodie.

Been There. Done That. Doing It Better!

I'm Not Old. I Just Got Here Before You Did.

If Things Get Better With Age, I'm Magnificent!

Who's Your Granddaddy?

Yes, I'm 92, But I Have the Body
Of a 78-Year-Old.

I May Be Old, But I Have the Stamina
Of a Man Twice My Age.

When There's Snow on the Roof,
There's Fire in the Furnace.

Age Is Only a Number, And Mine is Unlisted and Mostly Forgotten.

Support Bingo: Keep Grandma Off the Street.

At My Age, Everything Is an Extreme Sport.

It's Nice to Be Here. At My Age,
It's Nice to Be Anywhere.

I'm Young at Heart.
Other Parts of Me Are Slightly Older.

I'm Going South for the Winter.
Actually, Some Parts of Me
Are Headed There Already.

Nostalgia is Like a Grammar Lesson:
You Find the Present Tense, But the Past Perfect.

Nostalgia Isn't What It Used to Be.

It's Hard to Be Nostalgic
When You Can't Remember Anything.

Baby Boomers' Slogan:
Never Trust Anybody Over 90.

I Was at the Beauty Shop for Two Hours
—And That was Only for the Estimate.

Veni, Vidi, Velcro: I Came, I Saw, I Stuck Around.

I Intend to Live Forever. So Far, So Good.

That Snap, Crackle, and Pop
In the Morning Ain't My Rice Crispies.

When I Was Young, All I Wanted Was a Nice BMW.
Now, I Don't Care about the *W*.

I Was Always Taught to Respect My Elders.
It's Getting Harder and Harder to Find Them.

I'm Not 80 Years Old. I'm 26 Celsius.

CHAPTER 22

I May Be Old, But I'm Not Cold.

❦

At My Age, Flowers Scare Me.

❦

Live Each Day Like It's Your Last.
One Day You'll Get That Right.

❦

I Look Sharp—Like Carefully Aged Cheddar.

❦

With Age Comes Wisdom—and Discounts.

❦

Age Doesn't Always Bring Wisdom.
Sometimes Age Comes Alone.

❦

Age and Treachery Will Always
Defeat Youth and Skill.

❦

You *Can* Teach an Old Dog New Tricks.

❦

Brain Cells Come and Brain Cells Go,
But Fat Cells Last Forever.

❦

Do Old Men Wear Boxers or Briefs? Depends.

❦

Quit Worrying About Your Health. It'll Go Away.

❦

It's Not the Pace of Life That Concerns Me.
It's the Sudden Stop at the End.

❦

Hair Today. Gone Tomorrow.

❦

It Is Better to Wear Out Than to Rust Out.

❦

I Believe in Having Sex on the First Date.
At My Age, There May Not Be a Second One.

❦

Will Knit for Sex.

❦

Money Isn't Everything,
But It Sure Keeps the Grandkids in Touch.

I Used to Be a Scrabble Champion,
But I Became Inconsonant,
And I Can't Move My Vowels.

Incontinence Hotline: Can You Hold Please?

If You're Only As Old As You Feel,
How Can I Be Alive at 150?

We Went to Our 50th Reunion,
But Our Grandparents Showed Up.

I Don't Iron. I'm Not Wrinkle-Free,
So Why Should My Clothes Be?

I Support All Movements. I Eat Bran and Prunes.

Don't Let Aging Get You Down.
It's Too Hard to Get Back Up.

My Youth Was Misspent—
And My Old Age Is No Bargain Either.

Birthdays Are Like Chocolate:
The More You Have, the More They Show.

Be Still, My Beating Pacemaker.

Favorite Position for Seniors:
Face to Face; Separate Beds

I'm Still Hot. It Just Comes In Flashes Now.

Is It Just Me, Or Do High School Kids
Get Dumber and Dumber Every Year?

Avenge Yourself. Live Long Enough
To Be a Problem to Your Children.

23

Work Works

*I can't think of anything better to do with a life
than to wear it out in efforts to be useful to the world.*
–ARMAND HAMMER

$\mathcal{M}$ore and more seniors are staying in the American workforce well after the typical retirement age, some remaining in their pre-retirement fields and others going in a new direction. Some need the money, others want to try something new, and still others are just bored with traditional retirement and want to stay busy.

Whatever the reason, the number of seniors working past retirement age is growing fast and shows no sign of slowing down. In fact, the number of American workers over sixty-five will increase 80% in the next decade.

According to the U.S. Department of Labor, there are more than sixteen million Americans over age fifty-five who are either working (64% of them full time) or looking for jobs. AARP reports that 72% of all workers today plan to work after retirement, and 33% of all retirees reenter the job market within two years of retirement. The Social Security Administration predicts that, by 2020, the percentage of gainfully employed sixty-five to seventy-year-olds will be 30%, and of seventy to seventy-nine-year-olds 20%.

Research shows that seniors who participate in productive activities such as work have better physical and mental health, higher morale, and lower mortality rates. Whether work is a choice or a necessity, these seniors find they remain healthier longer, learn to be more open-minded and psychically mobile. They are more confident and less afraid of making mistakes and are willing to try new approaches to problem solving and productivity.

Work works for seniors in ways other than mental health and longevity. Older adults attached to the labor market have greater financial security by earning more money and by contributing to retirement plans for longer periods. A single man can approximately double his annual income level by retiring at age seventy instead of sixty-two. By working longer, many older workers also have prolonged access to medical insurance. By extending their working lives, seniors contribute more to the growth of local and state economies and rely less on public support services, such as Medicaid.

The benefits for businesses to retain knowledgeable and skilled mature workers can outweigh the costs of hiring new employees. In a number of surveys, chronologically gifted workers have been judged to be more cooperative, independent, knowledgeable, loyal, motivated, and patient than their younger colleagues. They are also more successful at gaining trust and communicating well with clients. And they are less likely to leave within ten days of training.

"Older workers not only see [retail] as an opportunity; they enjoy it," says Stephen Wing, director of workforce initiatives at CVS/Caremark. "They are dependable, and they act as mentors to younger staff—and the enthusiasm of young people can revitalize older workers." Replacing an experienced worker can cost a business 50% or more of the person's annual salary as well as institutional knowledge. Working seniors pass on their wisdom, knowledge, and experience to younger generations. In the process, these seniors live more fulfilling lives.

The Joys of Retirement

When a man retires
and time is no longer a matter of urgent importance,
his colleagues generally present him with a watch.
–R.C. SHERRIFF

Retire from work, but not from life.
–M.K. SONI

I believe the second half of one's life
is meant to be better than the first half.
The first half is finding out how you do it.
And the second half is enjoying it.
–FRANCES LEAR

Retirement has been a discovery of beauty for me.
I never had the time before to notice the beauty
of my grandkids, my wife,
the tree outside my very own front door.
And, the beauty of time itself.
–HARTMAN JULE

I've reached that time of life when I've finally added *re-* to *tired*—that time of life when I've stopped lying about my age and started lying about the house.

The other day my wife asked me, "What are you doing today?"

"Nothing, "I replied.

"But didn't you do that yesterday, too?" she asked.

"Yep, but I wasn't finished."

As an unrepentant retiree, I can tell you what I miss most about work—the vacations. I mean, when you retire, you never get a day off! And, I'm pleased to tell you, I don't need any.

Here's what my week looks like: Monday through Friday I do nothing, and on Saturday and Sunday I rest. I now have a new bedtime—three hours after I fall asleep on the couch. And currently my formal attire is long pants and tied shoes. And do you know what we retirees call a long lunch? Normal.

We retirees don't at all mind being called "senior citizens." That's because the term comes with a 10% discount. Sure we count our pennies. Because we are the only ones who have the time.

How many retirees does it take to change a light bulb? Only one, but it might take all day.

And here's what we retirees call people who enjoy work and refuse to retire: Nuts!

The Horrors of Retirement

I have always dreaded old age. I cannot imagine anything worse than being old. How awful it must be to have nothing to do all day long but stare at the walls or watch TV.

So last week, when the mayor suggested we all celebrate Senior Citizen Week by cheering up a senior citizen, I decided to call on my new neighbor. He was an elderly retired gentleman, recently widowed, who, I presumed, had moved in with his married daughter because he was too old to take care of himself. I baked a batch of brownies and without bothering to call (some old people cannot hear the phone), I went off to brighten this old fellow's day.

When I rang the doorbell, this "old fellow" came to the door dressed in tennis shorts and a polo shirt, looking about as ancient and decrepit as Donny Osmond.

"I'm sorry I can't invite you in," he said when I introduced myself, "but I'm due at the Racquet Club to play in the semifinals."

"Oh, that's all right," I said. "I baked you some brownies."

"Great!" he said, accepting the box, "Just what I need for bridge club tomorrow. Thanks so much!"

"I thought we'd visit a while, but that's okay, I'll just trot across the street and call on Granny Grady."

"Don't bother," he said. "Gran's not home. I just called to remind her of our date to go dancing tonight. She's off to the beauty parlor to get ready."

I called my mother's eighty-three-year-old cousin. She was in the hospital, working in the gift shop.

I called my seventy-four-year-old aunt. She was on vacation in China.

I called my husband's seventy-nine-year-old uncle. I'd forgotten that he was on his honeymoon.

I still dread old age, now more than ever. I just don't think I'm up to it. I'll never have enough time to get everything done.

Getting the Most Out of Retirement

Working people often ask my wife and me what we do to make our days interesting now that we're retired. Well, for example, yesterday my wife and I went to the mall to shop. When we came out, there was a police officer writing out a parking ticket. We approached him and I said, "Come on, man, how about giving a senior citizen a break?" He ignored us and continued writing the ticket.

I told him he had shown absolutely no respect for his elders. He glared at me and started writing another ticket for having worn tires.

Then my wife yelled at the officer that his parents had obviously done a rotten job of bringing him up. He finished the second ticket and put it on the windshield with the first. Then he started writing a third ticket. This went on for about twenty minutes. The more we abused him, the more tickets he wrote.

Just then our bus arrived. You see, the wife and I try to have a little fun each day now that we're retired. It's important at our age.

An Elementary View of Retirement

After Christmas break, a teacher asked her pupils how they spent their holidays. Here is one small boy's view of retirement in a mobile home park:

We always spent Christmas with grandma and grandpa. They used to live here in a big house, but grandpa got retarded and they moved to Florida. They live in a place with a lot of retarded people. They live in tin huts. They ride big tricycles that are too big for me.

They go to a big building they call a wreck hall. If it was wrecked, it is fixed now. They play games there and do exercises, but not very good. They play a game with big checkers and push them around on the floor with sticks.

There is a swimming pool there, and they go there just to stand in the water with their hats on. I guess they don't know how to swim.

My grandma used to make cookies and stuff, but I guess she forgot how. Nobody cooks there. They all go to restaurants that are fast and have discounts. They all go out for early bird specials. But I didn't eat any birds. I had eggs.

As you ride into the park, there is a dollhouse with a man sitting in it. He watches all day so they can't get out without him seeing them. They wear name badges with their names on them. I guess they all don't know who they are.

My grandma said grandpa worked hard all his life and earned retardment. I wish they would move back home, but I guess the man in the dollhouse won't let them.

Bumper Snickers for Retirement

Retirement Is the Best Medicine.

Goodbye Tension. Hello Pension.

**The Money's No Better in Retirement,
But the Hours Are.**

**Retired, Not Expired.
Distinguished, Not Extinguished.**

**I'm Retired. I Was Tired Yesterday,
And I'm Tired Again Today.**

**The Best Time to Think About Your Retirement
Is Before Your Boss Does.**

**My Wife Always Beats Me Up.
I'm Retired, and I Like to Sleep Late.**

Retirement: Half As Much Money,
Twice As Much Husband.

❧

I Wish That I Was Still Working—
That My Eyes Were Still Working,
My Back Was Still Working,
And My Knees Were Still Working.

❧

I'm Retired, and I'm So Busy That I Can't Figure Out
How I Ever Had Enough Time for Work.

The Importance of Exercise

I am pushing sixty. That is enough exercise for me.
–MARK TWAIN

Aging is natural, exercise is not.
Exercise is a lot like cleaning toilets.
It's something that needs to be done regularly,
but I like someone else to do it for me.
–CHARLOTTE LOBB

I have flabby thighs, but fortunately my stomach covers them.
–JOAN RIVERS

My doctor recently told me
that jogging could add years to my life.
I think he was right. I feel ten years older already.
–MILTON BERLE

We all get heavier as we get older because there's a lot more information in our heads. That's my story, and I'm sticking to it. When I was young, I used to go skinny dipping. Now I go chunky dunking. Actually, I've dropped a few pounds; or at least they've dropped on me—from my chest to my stomach and buttocks. I've managed to overcome my body issues the same way that I overcame my fear of heights: I simply don't look down.

I figure that if God wanted me to be able to touch my toes, He'd have put them on my knees. And I insist that the handle on my recliner counts as an exercise machine. Almost every day I stride briskly past a fitness center. Actually, I joined a health club last year and spent about $400 but I haven't lost a pound. Apparently you have to go there.

So I went there. I was told to wear loose-fitting clothes. Heck, if I had any loose-fitting clothing, I wouldn't have signed up in the first place.

A waist is a terrible thing to mind. I decided to take an aerobics class for seniors. I bent, twisted, gyrated, jumped up and down, and perspired for an hour. But by the time I got my leotard on, the class was over. Now that food has replaced sex in my life, I can't even get into my own pants.

I'm thinking of taking up walking so that I can hear heavy breathing again. I'll be sure to start my walk early in the morning—before my brain has figured out what I am doing. My grandfather started walking five miles a day when he was seventy-five. Now he's eighty-seven years old, and we still don't know where he is.

Every time I hear the dirty word *exercise*, I wash my mouth out with chocolate. Every time I feel the urge to exercise, I just lie down until it goes away. Every time I start thinking too much about how I look, I just find a Happy Hour, and by the time I leave, I look just fine.

Hey, there are only a certain number of beats that each heart has. Why would I want to use them up faster by exercising? But I do get a lot of exercise acting as a pallbearer for friends who exercise.

Seriously though, there are advantages of exercising every day: Exercise will enable me at eighty-five years old to spend an additional five months in a nursing home at $7,000 a month. When I die, they'll say, "Well, he looks good, doesn't he!"

Truth be told, I don't really need to exercise because I'm already in shape. I mean, round is a shape, isn't it?

15 Games for the Elderly

1. Sag, You're It
2. Peek-a-boo-I.C.U.
3. Pin the Toupee on the Bald Guy
4. Kick the Bucket
5. Musical Recliners
6. Olly, Olly, Oxidant Free
7. Marbles: Don't Lose Them
8. Shouting Down the Lane
9. Simon Says Something Incoherent
10. Hide and Go Sleep
11. Spin the Bottle of Mylanta
12. Doc Doc Goose Goose
13. Blind Man's LASIK Surgery
14. Ring Alleviate
15. Red Rover, Red Rover, the Nurse Says Bend Over

50 Exercises for Seniors

1. exercising your rights
2. beating around the bush
3. juggling your schedule
4. jogging your memory
5. jumping to conclusions
6. bending the rules
7. shooting the breeze
8. slinging mud
9. twisting someone's arm
10. bucking the system
11. carrying things too far
12. flying off the handle
13. climbing the walls
14. passing the buck
15. dodging responsibility
16. shaking a leg
17. throwing your weight around
18. dragging your heels
19. pushing your luck
20. adding fuel to the fire
21. fishing for compliments
22. starting the ball rolling
23. pulling strings

24. getting all shook up
25. raising cane
26. racking your brains
27. hitting the nail
    on the head
28. tossing in bed
29. turning the tables
30. wading through
    paperwork
31. shuffling papers
32. hopping
    on the bandwagon
33. balancing your checkbook
34. grappling with bills
35. wrestling with debt
36. fighting a cold

37. running around in circles
38. putting your foot
    in your mouth
39. falling in love
40. killing time
41. kicking yourself
42. splitting hairs
43. flipping TV channels
44. lifting an eyebrow
45. hiking up your trousers
46. opening a can of worms
47. striking a bargain
48. reaching retirement
49. spinning yarns
50. skipping exercise class

26

I'm So Old

I knew I was getting old when the Pope started looking young.
–BILLY WILDER

I have a wonderful make-up crew.
They're the same people restoring the Statue of Liberty.
–BOB HOPE

Back when I was a boy, I babysat for Grandma Moses—and for Moses.

Why, when I was a boy, General Motors, General Mills, and General Electric were just privates, Burger King was just a prince, Dairy Queen was just a princess, Madame Butterfly was a caterpillar, the Beatles were larvae, George H. W. Bush was a seedling, and Bigfoot wore a size-six shoe.

When I was a boy, the RCA Victor dog was just a puppy, Moby Dick was just a minnow, Godzilla was just a salamander, Avatars were Smurfs, and the Old Gray Mare was what she used to be. When I was a boy, Old Faithful was young and irresponsible, the Grand Canyon was a gopher hole, Old Smokey was a molehill, rainbows were in black and white—and the Dead Sea was only sick.

In fact, I'm so old that . . .
- My Social Security number is 1.
- I don't buy green bananas.

CHAPTER 26

- When I order a three-minute egg at a restaurant, they ask me for the money up front.
- My bank sends me its free calendar one month at a time.
- When I travel, I buy only one-way tickets.
- When I went to school, there wasn't any history class.
- My birth certificate, which is written on papyrus, has expired.
- My first driver's license, which is written in hieroglyphics, was for a chariot.
- Methuselah is in my high school yearbook.
- I see the faces of younger men on cash.
- Everything I see in antique stores and in museums I remember from my childhood.
- My first radio ran on gas.
- They've discontinued my blood type.
- Even my toupee has turned white.
- The average age of my friends is "deceased." I communicate with most of my friends through mediums and Ouija boards.
- All my friends in Heaven think I didn't make it.
- I can't remember how old I am.

27

Have You Heard?

Life before sixty is nothing but a warm-up.
–BILL HINSON

Have you heard about the elderly woman who was married to four husbands? Her first husband was an investment banker. The second was a movie star. The third was an evangelist. And the fourth was an undertaker.

You see, she wanted one for the money, two for the show, three to get ready, and four to go.

And have you heard about . . .

- the elderly statistician? *Eventually, she got broken down by age, sex, and marital status.*
- the elderly lion tamer? *His name was Whip Van Wrinkle.*
- the toothless senior who enjoyed eating lamb? *She licked her chops.*
- the elderly sea marauder? *His name was Graybeard the Pirate.*
- the elderly track-and-field judge? *She was an old timer.*
- the elderly population expert? *He took leave of his census.*

- the elderly accountant? *The more her figure grew the more she lost her balance.*
- the elderly lawyer? *He kept losing his appeal and expanding his briefs.*
- the elderly programmer? *She lost her memory.*
- the elderly rabbi? *He grew gray around the temples.*
- the fellow who insisted he felt like a young colt? *He looked more like an old .45.*
- the gold digger who performed magic? *She extracted mink from old goats and pearls from old crabs.*
- the elderly sailor? *He got a little dinghy.*
- the NBA team composed entirely of senior citizens? *They're called the Indiana Pacemakers.*
- the elderly Confederate general with fourteen children? *He had a lot of gray heirs.*
- the elderly rabbit couple? *They had a lot of gray hares.*
- the elderly dog? *He barked, "AARP! AARP!"*
- the elderly cat who became forgetful and stopped making any sounds? *She developed a purr-senility disorder.*
- the elderly, toothless grizzly? *She was a gummy bear.*
- the elderly, decrepit horse named Flattery? *It gets you nowhere.*
- the elderly kangaroo? *During his last years he was out of bounds.*
- the elderly skunk? *During his last years he made no scents at all.*

28

Seniors Under Attack!

I have everything I had twenty years ago
—except now it's all lower.
–GYPSY ROSE LEE

Maybe it's true that life begins at 50,
but everything else seems to wear out, fall out, or spread out.
–PHYLLIS DILLER

Something is happening right here in our own country!
We must stop this threat immediately!

Have you noticed that stairs are getting steeper?
Couches, chairs, and toilets have become lower. The arms
on airplane seats are now closer together, and the seat
belts are shorter. Groceries are heavier, and the lids on jars
are now epoxied. Everything is farther away. Yesterday I
walked to the corner and I was dumbfounded to discover
how long our street had become.

People are less considerate now, especially the young
ones. They speak in whispers all the time. If you ask them
to speak up, they just keep repeating themselves, endlessly
mouthing the same silent message until they're red in the
face! What do they think I am, a lip-reader?

People are much younger than I was at the same age.
On the other hand, people my own age are so much older
than I am. I ran into an old friend the other day, and she
had aged so much that she didn't even recognize me. I got

to thinking about the poor dear while I was combing my hair this morning, and in doing so, I glanced at my own reflection. Really now. Even mirrors are not made the way they used to be.

Another thing, everyone drives so fast these days! You're risking life and limb if you happen to pull onto the freeway in front of them. All I can say is, their brakes must wear out awfully fast, the way I see them screech and swerve in my rearview mirror.

Clothing manufacturers are less civilized these days. Why else would they suddenly start labeling a size 10 or 12 dress as 18 or 20? Do they think no one notices? The people who make bathroom scales are pulling the same prank. Do they think I actually believe the number I see on that dial? Ha! I would never let myself weigh that much! Just who do these people think they're fooling?

The conspiracy is deepening. Under cover of darkness, my thighs were stolen from me. One night I went to sleep in my body and woke up with someone else's thighs. The new ones had the texture of cooked oatmeal. Who would have done such a cruel thing to legs that had been mine for years? I spent the entire summer looking for my thighs. Hurt and angry, I am finally resigned to living out my life in jeans and Sheer Energy panty hose.

Then, just when my guard was down, the thieves struck again. My butt was next. I knew it was the same gang because they took pains to match my new rear end (although badly attached at least three inches lower than my original) to the thighs they stuck me with earlier. Now, my rear complemented my legs, lump for lump. Frantic, I prayed that long skirts would stay in fashion.

Next, my poor neck disappeared more quickly than the Thanksgiving turkey it now resembled. Then I realized my arms had been switched. One morning I was fixing my hair, and I watched horrified but fascinated as the flesh of my upper arms swung to and fro with the motion of the hairbrush. And somebody had made my arms shorter so that I could no longer read the newspaper.

This was really getting scary. My body was being replaced one section at a time. How fiendishly clever!

This is not a hoax. This is happening to women in every town every night. WARN YOUR FRIENDS! I'd like to call up someone in authority to report what's going on, but the telephone company is in on the conspiracy, too. They've printed the phone book in such small type that no one could ever find a number in there!

All I can do is broadcast this warning: WE ARE UNDER ATTACK! Unless something drastic happens, pretty soon everyone will have to suffer these awful indignities. Please pass this on to everyone you know as soon as possible so we can get this conspiracy stopped!

P.S. I am sending this to you in a larger font size because something has happened to my computer's fonts. Somebody has made them smaller!

P.P.S. I think I finally found my thighs. I hope that Angelina Jolie paid a really good price for them.

29

Jest for the Health of It

Old age ain't no place for sissies.
–BETTE DAVIS

Inside every seventy-year-old
is a thirty-five-year-old asking, "What happened?"
–ANN LANDERS

Don't talk to me about Valentine's Day.
At my age an affair of the heart is a bypass operation.
–JOAN RIVERS

My mother-in-law had a pain beneath her right breast.
It turned out to be a trick knee.
–PHYLLIS DILLER

After a certain age,
if you don't wake up aching in every joint,
you are probably dead.
–TOMMY MEIN

If you don't learn to laugh at trouble,
you won't have anything to laugh at when you grow old.
–EDGAR WATSON HOWE

You know you're growing old when . . .

- You finally get your head together, but your body falls apart.

- Your doctor doesn't give you X-rays anymore but just holds you up to the light.
- You sleep better on a reclining chair with the TV blaring than in bed.
- You lie awake many hours before your body allows you to get up.
- You now buy the large-type alphabet soup.
- You can get along without sex, but not without your glasses.
- You look for your glasses for a half an hour, and then discover that they were on your head all the time.
- You can't find your glasses without your glasses.
- The gleam in your eyes is the sun reflecting off your bifocals.
- You walk with your head held high, trying to get used to your trifocals.
- You choose your seat in the movie theater and the tour bus so that your good ear picks up the sound.
- What used to be your bad knee is now your good knee.
- You're in the initial stage of your golden years—*M.D., R.N., L.P.N.,* and *AARP.*
- You get winded playing chess, dialing long distance, and opening pill bottles.
- You sit in a rocking chair and can't get it going.
- You have contracted the dreaded furniture disease: Your chest has fallen into your drawers.
- Your knees buckle, but your belt won't.
- Your back goes out more than you do.
- You're willing to get up and give your seat to a lady–and can't.
- Your walker is equipped with an air bag.
- The answer to the question "Should I pee before I leave?" is always "Yes!"

CHAPTER 29

- You start making the same noises as your coffee maker.
- Even when you're naked, you want to slip into something more comfortable.

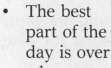

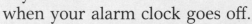

- The best part of the day is over when your alarm clock goes off.
- You sink your teeth into a steak and they stay there.
- You and your teeth don't sleep together.
- You dream about prunes.
- 6:00 AM is when you actually get up, not go to sleep.
- You feel that it's the morning after, when you haven't gone out the night before.
- You look both ways before crossing a room.
- Everything hurts, and what doesn't hurt doesn't work.
- Everything either dries up or leaks.
- Your freckles have become liver spots.
- Anything new you feel is probably a symptom.
- Conversations with people your own age often turn into "dueling ailments."
- Your most boring acquaintances are the ones who don't have anything wrong with them.
- You discover, while watching plays, movies, and television, that, while you're far too old to be a member of Generation X or Generation Y, you are a member of Generation Z-Z-Z-Z.

- People call at 9:00 AM and ask, "Did I wake you?"
- People call at 9:00 PM and ask, "Did I wake you?"
- The people who drive the electric carts in airports ask you if you need a ride.
- You have too much space in the house and not enough in the medicine cabinet.
- Half the stuff in your shopping cart says, "For Fast Relief."
- The bag boy in the "ten items or less" lane volunteers to help load groceries into your car.
- The pharmacist is your new best friend, and he or she hands you your prescriptions without asking for your name.
- Seeing the Little Dipper reminds you to take your Metamucil.
- Your weight-lifting program seems to have no effect on your muscles, but the veins on the backs of your hands are bulking up quite nicely.
- All your friends have thighs that touch each other.
- Your wild oats have turned into prunes and All-Bran.
- Your bones are getting softer, but your arteries are getting harder—so it all balances out.
- You depend on Allegra by day and Viagra by night.
- A dripping faucet causes an uncontrollable bladder urge.
- The wee hours have become the wee-wee hours.
- You go to the doctor with fluid on your knee, and he tells you that you're not aiming straight.
- Your hormone replacement therapy has to wait until all those other things in your body have been replaced.
- You can't remember the last time you didn't feel at least a little tired.
- You are always thinking that in a week or two you will feel better than ever.

Laughing at Our Infirmities

Youth thinks nothing of health. Age thinks of nothing else.
–EDMUND ORRIN

*My grandfather is hard of hearing. He needs to read lips.
I don't mind him reading lips,
but he uses one of those yellow highlighters.*
–BRIAN KILEY

*Have you not a moist eye?
a dry hand? a yellow cheek? a white beard?
a decreasing leg? an increasing belly?
Is not your voice broken? your wind short?
your chin double? your wits single?
and every part about you blasted with antiquity?*
–WILLIAM SHAKESPEARE, *KING HENRY IV, PART II*

*Eighty years old! No eyes left, no ears,
no teeth, no legs, no wind!
And when all is said and done,
how astonishingly well one does without them!*
–PAUL CLAUDEL

In ancient Greek mythology, the Sphinx posed one of the oldest known riddles in the world: "What animal walks on four feet in the morning, two at noon, and three in the evening?"

The hero Oedipus answered the riddle correctly: "Man. He crawls on all fours as a baby, walks on two feet when he is grown, and uses a cane in old age."

That cane comes with accessories—wrinkles, expanding waistlines, and achy-breaky body parts. But we can retaliate against our mortality by laughing at its side effects. "A merry heart doeth good like a medicine," the Bible tells us. Laughter galvanizes the circulation, tones the muscles, colors the cheeks, energizes the lungs and respiratory system, stimulates endorphins in the immune system, boosts the neurotransmitters needed for alertness and memory, increases motivation to learn, and provides superb aerobic exercise. Laughter can be hazardous to your infirmities.

Walk the Lines

During a visit with a friend at an assisted living center, a young man was invited to stay for lunch. As he entered the cafeteria with his host, she leaned toward him and whispered, "They have two lines here. We call them Cane and Able."

A Prescription for Success

Jacob, age ninety-two, and Rebecca, eighty-nine, were very excited about their decision to get married. They went for a stroll to discuss the wedding, and passed by a pharmacy. Jacob suggested they go inside. He went up to the pharmacist and said, "We're about to get married. Do you sell heart medication here?"

"Of course we do. This is a pharmacy."

"How about medicine for circulation?"

"All kinds."

"Medicine for rheumatism and scoliosis?"

"Definitely."

"How about Viagra?"

"That's one of our most popular items."

"Medicine for memory problems, arthritis, jaundice?"

"Yes, a large variety. The works."

"What about vitamins, sleeping pills, Geritol, antidotes for Parkinson's disease?"

"Absolutely."

"You sell wheelchairs and walkers?"

"All speeds and sizes."

Jacob then closed the conversation: "We'd like to use this store for our bridal registry."

Senioritis

Senior citizens constitute the fastest growing population acquiring AIDS—Band-Aids, hearing aids, walking aids . . .

Born Again

Two elderly gentlemen from a retirement center were sitting on a bench under a tree. One turned to the other and said, "Slim, I'm eighty-three years old now and I'm just full of aches and pains. I know you're about my age. How do you feel?"

Slim said, "I feel just like a newborn baby."

"Really? Like a newborn baby?"

"Yep. No hair. No teeth. I wake up every two hours and cry. And I think I just wet my pants."

Be Patient

A woman moved to a new city and went to see her new doctor. The doctor asked her how she was doing, so she gave him the litany of complaints: "This hurts, that's stiff, I'm tired and slower . . ."—on and on.

The doctor responded, "Mrs. Throckmorton, you have to expect things to start deteriorating. After all, who wants to live to a hundred?"

The patient looked him straight in the eye and replied, "Anyone who's ninety-nine."

Eh, What's That You Say?

Three retirees, each with a hearing loss, were taking a walk one fine March day. One remarked to the other, "Windy, ain't it?"

"No," the second man replied. "It's Thursday."

And the third man chimed in, "So am I. Let's have a soda."

Getting a Fair Hearing

An elderly gentleman had experienced serious hearing problems for a number of years. The man went to his doctor and was fitted with a set of hearing aids that allowed him to hear perfectly.

The elderly fellow went back in a month for a checkup, and the doctor observed, "Your hearing is flawless. Your family must be really pleased that you can hear again."

The gentleman replied, "Oh, I haven't told my family yet. I just sit around and listen to the conversations. I've changed my will three times."

Hear Here

The old man thought his wife was going deaf, so he came up behind her and asked, "Can you hear me, honey?"

No reply.

He spoke into her other ear, "Can you hear me, sweetheart?"

No reply.

The husband spoke louder, "Can you hear me, darling?"

His wife shouted, "For the third time, yes!"

Let's Get Physical

Eighty-two-year-old Morris went to the doctor to get a physical. A few days later, the doctor saw Morris walking down the street with a gorgeous young woman on his arm.

A week after that, the doctor spoke to Morris again. "How are you doing?" he asked.

Morris replied, "I'm doing just what you said, Doc: 'Get a hot mamma and be cheerful.'"

The doctor answered, "No. I said, 'You've got a heart murmur. Be careful.'"

The Joy of Sharing

In a fast-food restaurant, an elderly couple ordered one hamburger, one packet of fries, and one drink. The old man unwrapped the plain hamburger and carefully cut it in half, placing one half in front of his wife. He then carefully counted out the fries, dividing them into two piles and neatly placing one portion in front of his wife.

He took a sip of the drink, his wife took a sip, and then he set the cup down between them.

As he began to eat his few bites of hamburger, the people around them kept looking over and whispering, "That poor old couple. All they can afford is one meal for the two of them."

As the man began to eat his fries, a young woman came to the table. She politely offered to buy another meal for the old couple. The old man replied that they were just fine, but they were just used to sharing everything.

The surrounding people noticed the little old lady hadn't eaten a bite. She sat there watching her husband eat and occasionally took turns sipping the drink.

A young man came over and begged them to let him buy another meal for them. The old woman said, "No, thank you, sir. We are used to sharing everything."

As the old man finished and wiped his face neatly with the napkin, several customers came over to the little old lady who had yet to eat a single bite of food and inquired, "May we ask what is it you are waiting for?"

The old woman answered, "The teeth."

My Forgetter Is Getting Better

My memory is starting to go.
The only thing I still retain is water.
–ALEX COLE

My grandmother is eighty-five years old,
and she's starting to lose her memory.
Everybody's upset about it except me
Because I got eight checks from her for my birthday.
Hey, that's forty bucks.
–TOM ARNOLD

*A*t my age, I've seen everything, I've heard everything, and I've done everything. Unfortunately, at my age, I can't remember any of it. My mind not only wanders. Sometimes it goes away completely.

I think I may be losing my memory. Also, I think I may be losing my memory.

The preacher came to visit me the other day. He said at my age, I should be thinking about "the hereafter."

I told him, "Oh, I do, all the time! No matter where I am—in the parlor, upstairs, in the kitchen, or down in the basement—I ask myself, "Now what am I here after?"

Somebody has revoked my remembership in life. I used to drink to forget. Now I don't have to drink. I'm not having a senior moment. I'm having a senior decade.

I used to have a photographic memory, but I seem to have misplaced the film. I also can't find my family book of memorabilia. I'm a walking storehouse of facts, but I seem to have misplaced the key to the door. I also forget where I put my family book of memorabilia.

I do know there are three signs of old age. The first is memory loss. I forget the other two. For example, I have trouble remembering basic words like . . . um . . . But I always remember my kids' names, just not always the right ones. And I remembered this week that last week was my wedding anniversary.

I keep repeating myself. I keep repeating myself. I keep repeating myself.

I get a hundred pages into a book before I realize I've read it before.

I may be a victim of Mallzeimer's Disease. I stand in a mall trying to remember why I came and where I parked your car. That's why I use a lot more valet parking, because valets remember where they parked my car.

In tennis, I now prefer doubles to singles because there's a better chance that somebody on the court will remember the score. And I always play golf in a foursome for the same reason.

But there are many advantages to losing my memory: I may not go anywhere, but I constantly meet new people and hear new jokes—even if they're the same ones I met and heard the day before. I have a few good jokes in my own repertoire, but I can't recall which people I've told them to. You could say I'm in my anecdotage. And my secrets are safe with my friends because they can't remember my secrets.

My Forgetter

My forgetter's getting better,
But my rememberer is broke.
To you that may seem funny,
But, to me, that is no joke.

For when I'm "here," I'm wondering
If I should instead be "there,"
And, when I try to think it through,
I haven't got a prayer!

At times I walk into a room,
Say, "What am I here for?"
I wrack my brain, but all in vain.
A zero is my score.

At times I put something away
Where it is safe, but, gee,
The person it is safest from
Is generally me!

When shopping, I may see someone
And stop and have a chat.
Then, when the person leaves, I ask,
"Now who the heck was that?"

Yes, my forgetter's getting better
While my rememberer is broke,
And it's driving me plumb crazy
And that isn't any joke.

Out of Mind, Out of Sight

"How was your golf game, dear?" asked Murray's wife.

"I was hitting the ball pretty well, but my eyesight's gotten so bad I couldn't see where the ball went."

"Look, you're seventy-five years old, Murray," his wife explained. "Why don't you take my brother Ira along?"

"But he's eight-five and doesn't even play golf anymore," Murray protested.

"But Ira's got perfect eyesight. He could watch your ball."

The next day Murray teed off, with Ira looking on. Murray swung, and the ball disappeared down the middle of the fairway.

"Did you see the ball?" asked Murray.

"Yep," Ira answered.

"Where is it?" yelled Murray, peering off into the distance.

"I forget."

A Change of Mind

A group of forty-year-old buddies agreed that they should get together for dinner. They debated where to gather and finally decided to meet at the Godfrey Gardens Restaurant because the waitresses there were cute and wore low-cut outfits.

THE GIFT OF AGE

Ten years later, at fifty, the pals decided to meet for a dinner together. They chose Godfrey Gardens because the food and wine selection there was great.

A decade after that, the sixty-year-olds again agreed to have their reunion at Godfrey Gardens because they could dine there in peace and quiet, and the restaurant was smoke-free.

When the aging buddies turned seventy, they came up with a plan to join each other at Godfrey Gardens because the restaurant offered senior discounts, was wheelchair accessible, and had an elevator.

At eighty years of age, the longtime friends agreed that it would be a great idea to have dinner together at Godfrey Gardens because they'd never eaten there before.

Sister Act

Three sisters, ages eighty-six, eighty-eight, and ninety, lived in a house together. One night the ninety-year-old drew a bath. She put her foot in, paused, and called out to her sisters, "Was I getting in or out of the bath?"

The eighty-eight-year-old yelled back, "I don't know. I'll come up and see." She started up the stairs and paused. "Was I going up the stairs or down?" she asked.

The eighty-six-year-old was sitting at the kitchen table having tea and listening to her sisters. She shook her head and said, "I sure hope I never get that forgetful, knock on wood." Then she yelled, "I'll come up and help both of you as soon as I see who's at the door."

On the Same Page

A couple in their nineties were both having problems remembering things. During a checkup, the doctor told them that they were physically okay, but they might want to start writing things down to help them remember.

Later that night, while they watched TV, the old man got up from his chair. "Want anything while I'm in the kitchen?" he asked his wife.

"Will you get me a bowl of ice cream?"

"Sure."

"Don't you think you should write it down so you can remember it?" she asked.

"No, I can remember it."

"Well, I'd like some strawberries and whipped cream on top, too. Maybe you should write it down so you don't forget it."

Irritated, he said, "I don't need to write it down, I can remember it! Ice cream with strawberries and whipped cream—I got it, for goodness sake!" Then he doddered into the kitchen.

After about twenty minutes, the old man returned from the kitchen and handed his wife a plate of bacon and eggs.

She stared at the plate for a moment. "Where's my toast?"

Oh Dear

An old fellow was sitting on a park bench weeping uncontrollably. A young man walked by and asked what was wrong.

"I'm married to a gorgeous twenty-five-year-old woman, who gives me anything I ask for," said the old man.

"What's wrong with that?"

"I forget where I live."

But Seriously . . .

"Think of your brain as a library in which you are looking for a particular book. If it is a young library with only a few books, the one you seek will be easy to find. If it is an older library full of thousands of books, finding a particular book will take longer. But the book is still there if you will take the time to look for it. Patience may be required to locate a certain book in a large and full library."–*Vicki Schmall* and *Clara Pratt*

AAADD

Old age is not a disease.
It is strength and survivorship, triumph over all kinds
of vicissitudes and disappointments, trials and illnesses.
–MAGGIE KUHN

I wake up in the morning,
and it takes me a half-hour to find my glasses,
just so I can look for my teeth,
to tell my wife to find my hair.
–RICHARD JENNI

Recently, I was diagnosed with AAADD—Age Activated Attention Deficit Disorder. Even though I have it, I feel much better now that I know it has a name. Here's how it manifests:

I decide to water my garden. As I turn on the hose in the driveway, I look over at my car and decide it needs washing. As I start toward the garage, I notice mail on the porch table that I brought up from the mailbox earlier. I decide to go through the mail before I wash the car. I lay my car keys on the table, put the junk mail in the garbage can under the table, and notice that the can is full.

So . . . I decide to put the bills back on the table and take out the garbage first. But then I think, since I'm going to be near the mailbox when I take out the garbage anyway, I might as well pay the bills first. I take my checkbook off the table and see that there is only one check left. My extra checks are in my desk in the study, so I go inside the house to my desk where I find the can of soda I'd been drinking.

I'm going to look for my checks, but first I need to push the soda aside so that I don't accidentally knock it over. The soda is getting warm, so I decide to put it in the refrigerator to keep it cold. As I head toward the kitchen with the soda, a vase of flowers on the counter catches my eye. They need water.

I put the soda on the counter and discover my reading glasses that I've been searching for all morning. I decide that I better put them back on my desk—but first I'm going to water the flowers. I set the glasses back down on the counter, fill a container with water, and suddenly spot the TV remote somebody must have left on the kitchen table.

I realize that tonight when I go to watch TV, I'll be looking for the remote, but I won't remember that it's on the kitchen table, so I decide to put it back in the den, where it belongs, but first I'll water the flowers. I pour some water in the flowers, but quite a bit of it spills on the floor. So I set the remote back on the table, get some towels, and wipe up the spill. Then, I head down the hall trying to remember what I was planning to do.

At the end of the day, the car isn't washed, the bills aren't paid, a warm can of soda sits on the counter, the flowers don't have enough water, there's still only one check in my checkbook, and I can't find the remote, my glasses, or the car keys.

When I try to figure out why nothing got done today, I'm baffled because I know I was busy all day and I'm really pooped.

I realize this is a serious problem, and I'll try to get some help for it. But first I need to check my e-mail.

The Letter

Just a line to say I'm living,
That I'm not among the dead,
Though I'm getting more forgetful.
Things are falling from my head.

I got used to my arthritis,
To my dentures I'm resigned.
I can manage my bifocals,
But I really miss my mind.

For sometimes I can't remember,
When I stand atop the stairs,
If I must go down for something
Or I've just come up from there.

And before the fridge, so often,
My mind is filled with doubt.
Have I just put the food away,
Or come to take some out?

I called a friend not long ago.
When they answered, I just moaned.
I hung up without speaking,
I'd forgotten whom I'd phoned.

When the darkness falls upon me,
I stand and scratch my head.
I don't know if I'm retiring,
Or just getting out of bed.

Once I stood in my own bathroom,
Wondering if I'd used the pot.
I flushed it just in case I had
And sat down in case I'd not.

If it's now my turn to write you,
There's no need for getting sore.
It may be I think I've written
And don't need to write no more.

Now I stand beside the mailbox
With a face so very red.
Instead of mailing you the letter,
I have opened it instead.

Ripe Love

The older the violin, the sweeter the music
—CURLY PUTMAN

*An archaeologist is the best husband a woman can have.
The older she gets the more interested he is in her.*
—AGATHA CHRISTIE

*Oh, the days dwindle down
To a precious few . . .
And these few precious days
I'll spend with you.*
—MAXWELL ANDERSON, *SEPTEMBER SONG*

*One of the best parts of growing older?
You can flirt all you like since you've become harmless.*
—LIZ SMITH

Sex at ninety is like trying to shoot pool with a rope.
—GEORGE BURNS

The Four Stages of Sex Life

1. Tri-weekly

2. Try weekly.

3. Try weakly.

4. Try, try, try.

The Secret

A couple in their eighties was celebrating their sixtieth wedding anniversary. Not surprisingly, they were asked the secret of their long marriage.

Explained the husband: "Early in our marriage, we agreed that we would never go to bed angry. And the longest we've ever stayed awake is five days."

Car Chase

A woman saw her elderly husband flirting with a younger woman at a party. The wife remarked to a friend, "He's like a dog chasing cars. He wouldn't know what to do if he caught one."

May Becomes December

Milton, a seventy-year-old extremely wealthy widower, showed up at his country club with a breathtakingly beautiful and very sexy twenty-five-year-old blonde. The young woman knocked everyone's socks off with her youthful appeal and outright charm while hanging on Milton's arm and listening intently to his every word. His buddies at the club were all flabbergasted. They cornered him and asked, "Milton, how did you manage to attract such an amazing-looking trophy girlfriend?"

Milton replied, "Girlfriend? She's my wife!"

"Incredible! How did you persuade her to marry you?"

"I lied about my age," Milton explained.

"What do you mean? Did you tell her you were only fifty?"

Milton smiled and said, "No, I told her I was ninety."

A Hot and Cold Relationship

After an examination, the doctor said to his elderly patient, "You appear to be in good health. Do you have any medical concerns you would like to ask me about?"

"In fact, I do," answered the old man. "After my wife and I have sex, I'm usually cold and shivering. And then, after I have sex with her the second time, I'm usually hot and sweaty."

When the doctor examined the man's elderly wife a short time later, he asked, "Everything appears to be fine. Are there any medical concerns that you would like to discuss with me?"

The lady replied that she had no questions or concerns, leading the doctor to ask, "Your husband mentioned an unusual problem. He claimed that he was usually cold and shivering after having sex with you the first time and then hot and sweaty after the second time. Do you have any idea about why?"

"I think I do know why," the wife explained. "It's because the first time is usually in January, and the second time is in August."

Rethinking His Priorities

After thirty years of marriage, a man looked at his wife one day and said, "You know, thirty years ago we lived in a cheap apartment, drove a clunker of a car, watched a small black-and-white television, and slept in a sofa bed. But every night I got to sleep with a hot twenty-five-year-old blonde.

"Now, after thirty years of hard work," he continued, "we have a nice house, a luxurious car, a big flat-screen TV, and a king-size bed—but I have to sleep with a fifty-five-year-old woman. It doesn't seem fair."

His wife, a reasonable woman, replied, "Well, why don't you go out and get yourself a hot twenty-five-year-old blonde? Then I'll make sure that you once again live in a cheap apartment, drive a clunker of a car, watch a small black-and-white television, and sleep in a sofa bed."

Guess what the man decided to do.

With Age Comes Wisdom

An eighty-year-old man was sitting in his fishing boat when he heard a voice call out, "Pick me up!"

He looked in the water and there, frog-kicking on the surface, was a frog. "Are you talking to me?" asked the man.

"Yes, I'm talking to you," replied the frog. "Pick me up and kiss me, and I'll turn into the most beautiful young woman you have ever seen. I'll make sure that all your friends are envious and jealous because I will be your bride!"

The man looked at the frog for a short time, reached over, picked it up carefully,

and placed it in his front breast pocket. "What are you, nuts?" screamed the frog. "Didn't you hear what I said? Kiss me and I will be your beautiful bride!"

Good Morning!

The old fellow opened his pocket, looked at the frog, and said, "Nah, at my age I'd rather have a talking frog."

The Dating Game

An eighty-three-year-old widow went on a blind date with a ninety-year-old man. When she returned to her daughter's house late that evening, she seemed upset. "What happened, Mother?" asked the daughter.

"I had to slap his face three times!"

"You mean he got fresh with you?"

"No," answered the mother. "I thought he was dead."

True Confessions

An elderly man walked into a confessional. He said to the priest behind the screen, "I'm seventy-five years old and have been dating three twenty-year-olds."

"Well, they're awfully young for you, but what you're doing is not a sin," the priest responded.

"I didn't come here to talk about my sins, Father. I'm Jewish."

"You're Jewish! Why have you come here to tell me all this?"

"I'm seventy-five years old. I'm telling everybody!"

Fresh Man

Two elderly gentlemen were shooting the breeze. "I guess you're never too old," the first one boasted. "Why just yesterday a pretty college girl said she'd be interested in dating me, but to be perfectly honest, I don't quite understand it."

"Well," said his friend, "you have to remember that nowadays women are more aggressive. They don't mind being the one to ask."

"No, I don't think it's that."

"Well, maybe you remind her of her father."

"No, it's not that either. It's just that she also mentioned something about carbon-14."

144

You know you're growing old when...

- You see a pretty young girl and wonder what her mother looks like.
- The pretty girl you smile at thinks you are one of her father's friends. And she helpfully opens the door for you.
- When you whistle at a pretty girl, she thinks you're calling her dog.
- All your dreams about girls are reruns.
- The little gray-haired lady you help across the street is your wife.
- When you see a pretty girl, your pacemaker makes the garage door open.
- When you have a choice of temptations, you choose the one that gets you home earlier.
- Dinner and a movie are the whole date, not just the start of one.
- You're getting better in bed. You can sleep there for days.
- Your wife tells you she's having an affair, and you ask if she's having it catered.
- Your sweetie says, "Let's go upstairs and make love," and you answer, "Pick one. I can't do both."
- Your sweetie says, "Would you like some super sex?" and you say, "I'll take the soup."

Auto Biographies

My Nana: ninety years old and still driving.
Not with me. That would be stupid.
–TIM ALLEN

Mario Andretti has retired from racecar driving.
That's a good thing. He's getting old.
He ran his entire last race with his left blinker on.
–JON STEWART

When I die, I want to die like my grandfather did—
peacefully in his sleep.
Not screaming like all the passengers in his car.
–AUTHOR UNKNOWN

Looking on the Bright Side

I've sure gotten old. I've had two bypass surgeries, a hip replacement, and new knees. I've fought prostate cancer and diabetes. I'm half blind, can't hear anything quieter than a jet engine, take forty different medications that make me dizzy, winded, am subject to blackouts, and I wrestle with bouts of dementia. My circulation is so sluggish that I can hardly feel my hands and feet anymore. My memory's gone; I'm not even sure of my age. But thank my lucky stars, I still have my Florida driver's license.

CHAPTER 34

Driving Miss Hazy

Two elderly sisters were out driving. As they were cruising along, they came to an intersection. The stoplight was red, but they just went right on through. The sister in the passenger seat thought to herself "I must be losing it. I could have sworn we just went through a red light."

A few minutes later they came to another intersection, and again they went right through. The sister in the passenger seat was almost sure that the light had been red, but was really concerned that she was losing it.

At the next intersection, sure enough, the light was red, and again they sailed right through. So the passenger turned to her sister and said, "Mildred, did you know that we just ran through three red lights in a row? You could have killed us both!"

Mildred turned to her sister and asked, "Oh! Am I driving?"

My Way on the Highway

As a senior citizen was driving down the freeway, his car phone rang. Answering, he heard his wife's voice urgently warning him, "Herman, I just heard on the news that there's a car going the wrong way on 280. Please be careful!"

"Heck," said Herman, "It's not just one car. It's hundreds of them!"

A Likely Story

A chronologically endowed woman was speeding down the highway, when a young officer stopped her automobile. She looked him in the eye and explained, "Officer, I had to get somewhere in a hurry before I forgot where I was going."

He let her off.

A Conversation Between Two Oldsters

"So I hear you're getting married?"

"Yep!"

"This woman, is she good looking?"

"Not really."

"Is she a good cook?"

"Naw, she can't cook too well."

"Does she have lots of money?"

"Nope! Poor as a church mouse."

"Well, then, is she good in bed?"

"I wouldn't know."

"Why in the world do you want to marry her then?"

"Because she can still drive at night!"

But seriously . . .

Despite the stereotypes that animate the jokes in this chapter, a 2010 study by the Insurance Institute for Highway Safety revealed that the chronologically endowed are driving more and driving better. The fatal crash rate for seniors has plummeted 37%, with the biggest drop of all—47%—coming for drivers above the age of eighty.

The researchers compared the performance of older drivers with a control group whose members spanned thirty-five to fifty-four years of age. The chronologically gifted drivers did far better than the control group. Possible reasons for this improved report card for seniors include better health, safer cars, and increased screening of and more informed self restriction by older drivers.

Ad-Vintage

Age does not wither her,
nor custom stale her infinite variety.
–WILLIAM SHAKESPEARE, *ANTONY AND CLEOPATRA*

My parents didn't want to move to Florida,
but they turned sixty and that's the law.
–JERRY SEINFELD

Words That Don't Ad Up

These addled ads actually appeared in newspapers:

- The license fee for altered dogs with a certificate will be three dollars and for pets owned by seniors who have not been altered the fee will be a dollar-fifty.
- The Macon County Humane Society offers a free spay/neutering to senior citizens if they adopt an animal out of the animal shelter.
- Atkins Photo Studio is now shooting seniors for free.
- Armadale Dry Cleaners. Specializing in Wedding Dresses, Graduation Gowns, Baptismal Gowns. Discount for Seniors
- FOR SALE: Lady's chest with thick legs and large drawers. 101 years old. Perfect for antique lover.
- Widow, 73, would like to meet gent with car of similar age.
- Elderly woman seeks female to share house and perform cleaning and some nursing assistance. Must be a nonsmoker and drinker.

Classified Classics

The following personal ads were posted in Florida and Arizona newspapers. Who says seniors don't have a sense of humor?

- Male, 1922, high mileage, good condition, some hair, many new parts including hip, knee, cornea, valves. Isn't in running condition, but walks well.

- Recent widow who has just buried fourth husband looking for someone to round out a six-unit plot. Dizziness, fainting, shortness of breath not a problem.

- I am into solitude, long walks, sunrises, the ocean, yoga, and meditation. If you are the silent type, let's get together, take our hearing aids out, and enjoy quiet times.

- Active grandmother with original teeth seeking a dedicated flosser to share rare steaks, corn on the cob, and caramel candy.

- I still like to rock, still like to cruise in my Camaro on Saturday nights, and still like to play the guitar. If you were a groovy chick, or are now a groovy hen, let's get together and listen to my eight-track tapes.

- Sexy, fashion-conscious blue-haired beauty, 80's, slim, 5' 4" (used to be 5' 6"), searching for sharp-looking, sharp-dressing companion. Matching white shoes and belt a plus.

- I can usually remember Monday through Thursday. If you can remember Friday, Saturday, and Sunday, let's put our two heads together.

- 80-year-old bubby, no assets, seeks handsome, virile Jewish male under 35. Object matrimony. I can dream, can't I?

- *Wanted:* Bonded escort, silver-haired (not dyed), two days a week for three active ladies eighty-plus. Should look rich (but not too rich). Politically conservative. Good bridge player and waltzer. Sharp enough to handle six Bingo cards at once. Prefer chauffeur's license, LPN, and Black Belt in karate.

A Senior's Night Before Christmas

(with thanks to Clement Clarke Moore)

'Twas the night before Christmas at Rock-Away Rest,
And all of us seniors were looking our best.
Our glasses, how sparkly, our wrinkles, how merry.
The punchbowl held prune juice plus three drops of sherry.

A bedsock was taped to each walker, in hope
That Santa would bring us soft candy and soap.
We surely were lucky to be there with friends,
Secure in this residence and our Depends.

THE GIFT OF AGE

Our grandkids had sent us some Christmasy crafts,
Like angels in snowsuits and penguins on rafts.
The dental assistant had borrowed our teeth,
And from them she'd crafted a holiday wreath.

The bedpans, so shiny, all stood in a row,
Reflecting our candles' magnificent glow.
Our supper so festive—the joy wouldn't stop.
'Twas creamy warm oatmeal with sprinkles on top.

Our salad was Jell-O, so jiggly and great.
A puree of fruitcake was spooned on each plate.
The Social Director then had us play games,
Like "Where Are You Living?" and "What Are Your Names?"

Security lights on the new fallen snow
Made outdoors seem noon to the old folks below.
Then out on the porch there arose quite a clatter—
But we are so deaf that it just didn't matter.

A strange little fellow flew in through the door,
Then tripped on the sill and fell flat on the floor.
'Twas just our Director, all togged out in red.
He jiggled and chuckled and patted each head.

We knew from the way that he strutted and jived
Our Social Security checks had arrived.
We sang—how we sang—in our monotone croak,
Till the clock tinkled out its soft 8:00 PM stroke.

And soon we were snuggling deep in our beds,
While nurses distributed nocturnal meds.
And so ends our Christmas at Rock-Away Rest.
Soon you will be with us. We wish you the best!

A Good Old Game

*The most aggravating thing about the younger generation
is that I no longer belong to it.*
–ALBERT EINSTEIN

You might think that anything to do with the word *old* is the same old, same old—old fashioned, old hat, old school, and old guard, old as the hills, old as Methuselah, and older than dirt. But *old* appears in a surprisingly large number of titles, places, brand names, expressions, and the like. From the clues that follow, identify each that contains a form of the word *old*:

Americana

1. the United States flag 2. a nickname for the U. S. frigate Constitution 3. a nickname for Andrew Jackson
4. a nickname for Zachary Taylor 5. a geyser in Yellowstone Park 6. where Wild Bill Hickok and Jesse James lived 7. Europe and Asia, compared to the Americas

Entertainment

8. movie comedy starring Jack Lemmon and Walter Matthau 9. Best Motion Picture in 2007 10. public television show 11. a weekly country music show broadcast from Nashville 12. a famous Disney dog 13. a nickname for Frank Sinatra 14. a London theater company 15. protagonist of "Peanuts"

Songs

16. classic songs 17. what to "tie a yellow ribbon round" 18. That "music just soothes the soul." 19. It's "with a different meaning since you've been gone." 20. She's "from Pasadena." 21. It's "got nothin' to do but roll around Heaven all day." 22. a mountain "covered with snow" 23. It's the moon "in your eyes." 24. the Mississippi 25. when "she's your tootsy-wootsy" 26. what "school days, school days" were 27. He "had a farm." 28. She "ain't what she used to be." 29. She "swallowed a fly." 30. He "is snoring." 31. He "came rolling home." 32. What you should "go tell Aunt Rhody." 33. "It's good enough for me." 34. "the emblem of suffering and shame" 35. Scottish for "long time ago"

Songs by Stephen Foster

36. that in which "the sun shines bright" 37. what "I hear those gentle voices calling" 38. "ever-faithful" dog 39. This song begins "Way down upon de Swanee Ribber."

Literature

40. the first part of the Christian Bible 41. a novel by Charles Dickens 42. a novel by Ernest Hemingway 43. *Arsenic and _____* 44. He "called for his fiddlers three." 45. She "lived in a shoe." 46. She "went to the cupboard." 47. a yearly publication out of Dublin, New Hampshire

Higher Education

48. a university in Oxford, Mississippi 49. a university in Norfolk, Virginia 50. that extra effort

Commercial Products

51. a defunct automobile brand 52. a deodorant brand 53. a cleanser brand 54. a national department store chain 55. a national restaurant chain

CHAPTER 37

Expressions

56. an adage 57. superstitious stories spread from one generation to the next 58. what you can't teach new tricks 59. where a chip comes from 60. where people customarily gather 61. one thing a bride carries 62. They "never die."

Answers

1. Old Glory 2. Old Ironsides 3. Old Hickory 4. Old Rough and Ready 5. Old Faithful 6. the Old West 7. the Old World

8. *Grumpy Old Men* 9. *No Country for Old Men* 10. *This Old House* 11. Grand Ole Opry 12. Old Yeller 13. Old Blue Eyes 14. The Old Vic 15. good old Charlie Brown

16. golden oldies, old standards 17. the old oak tree 18. that old time rock and roll 19. the same old song 20. the little old lady 21. that lucky old sun 22. Old Smokey 23. that old devil moon 24. Old Man River 25. in the good old summertime 26. dear old golden-rule days 27. Old McDonald 28. the old gray mare 29. an old lady 30. the old man 31. this old man 32. the old gray goose is dead 33. that old-time religion 34. "The Old Rugged Cross" 35. "Auld Lang Syne"

36. "My old Kentucky home" 37. "Old Black Joe" 38. "old dog Tray" 39. "Old Folks at Home"

40. the Old Testament 41. *The Old Curiosity Shop* 42. *The Old Man and the Sea* 43. *Old Lace* 44. Old King Cole 45. an old lady 46. Old Mother Hubbard 47. *The Old Farmer's Almanac*

48. Old Miss 49. Old Dominion 50. the old college try

51. Oldsmobile 52. Old Spice 53. Old Dutch Cleanser 54. Old Navy 55. The Old Spaghetti Factory

56. an old chestnut, an old saw 57. old wives' tales 58. an old dog 59. the old block 60. the old stamping grounds 61. something old 62. old soldiers

Never Say Die

Musicians don't retire.
They stop when there's no more music in them.
–LOUIS AMSTRONG

It ain't over till it's over.
–YOGI BERRA

When General Douglas MacArthur retired from the military in 1951, he declaimed the famous line "Old soldiers never die—they just fade away." But five-star generals are not the only ones who never say die:

- Old librarians never die—they just check out, become overdue, and lose their circulation.
- Old crossword puzzlers never die—they just go across and up.
- Old milkmaids never die—they just kick the bucket and lose their whey.
- Old plumbers never die—they just get out of sink and go down the drain.
- Old teachers never die—they just grade away and lose their principals, their faculties, and their class.
- Old math professors never die—they just go off on a tangent.
- Old mimes never die—they're just never heard from again.

CHAPTER 38

- Old housemaids never die—they just return to dust.
- Old classicists never die—they just keep declining.
- Old can collectors never die—they just go to the redemption center.
- Old welders never die—they just pass the torch.
- Old candlemakers never die—they just get snuffed out.
- Old cartoonists never die—they just draw their last breath and go into a state of suspended animation.
- Old gangsters never die—they just go to the underworld.
- Old bikers never die—they just get recycled.
- Old Egypt tourists never die—they just go senile and meet their mummies.
- Old calliope players never die—they just run out of steam.
- And, of course, old movie stars never die—they just fade away.

Had enough? No? Good. Fill in each blank in this die-hard quiz. Suggested answers follow.

1. Old quarterbacks never die—they just fade back and _____ away.
2. Old skiers never die—they just go _____.
3. Old Australians never die—they just end up _____.
4. Old tree surgeons never die—they just pine away and take a final _____.
5. Old sausage makers never die—they just take a turn for the _____.
6. Old bricklayers never die—they just throw in the _____.
7. Old logicians never die—they just vacate the _____.

8. Old hairdressers never die—they just curl up and _____ .

9. Old florists never die—they just rest on their _____ .

10. Old clockmakers never die—they just get _____ .

Answers
1. pass 2. downhill 3. Down Under 4. bough
5. wurst 6. trowel 7. premises 8. dye 9. laurels
10. run down (and ticked off)

39

Golden Poetry

To every thing there is a season,
and a time to every purpose under Heaven.
–ECCLESIASTES 3:1

For Age is not alone of time, or we should never see
Men old and bent at forty and men young at seventy-three.
–EDGAR GUEST

When You Are Old

When you are old and grey and full of sleep,
And nodding by the fire, take down this book,
And slowly read, and dream of the soft look
Your eyes had once, and of their shadows deep;

How many loved your moments of glad grace,
And loved your beauty with love false or true,
But one man loved the pilgrim soul in you,
And loved the sorrows of your changing face;

And bending down beside the glowing bars,
Murmur, a little sadly, how Love fled
And paced upon the mountains overhead
And hid his face amid a crowd of stars.

–William Butler Yeats

Morituri Salutamus

What then? Shall we sit idly down and say
The night hath come; it is no longer day?
The night hath not yet come; we are not quite
Cut off from labor by the failing light;
Something remains for us to do or dare;
Even the oldest tree some fruit may bear;

. . .

For age is opportunity no less
Than youth itself, though in another dress,
And as the evening twilight fades away
The sky is filled with stars, invisible by day.

–Henry Wadsworth Longfellow

Sonnet 73

That time of year thou mayst in me behold
When yellow leaves, or none, or few, do hang
Upon those boughs which shake against the cold,
Bare ruin'd choirs, where late the sweet birds sang.

In me thou see'st the twilight of such day
As after sunset fadeth in the west;
Which by and by black night doth take away,
Death's second self, that seals up all in rest.

In me thou see'st the glowing of such fire
That on the ashes of his youth doth lie,
As the death-bed whereon it must expire,
Consumed with that which it was nourish'd by.

This thou perceivest, which makes thy love more strong,
To love that well which thou must leave ere long.

–William Shakespeare

40

Movie Stars on Aging

- The hardest years in life are those between ten and seventy.–*Helen Hayes* (at seventy-three)
- Old age isn't so bad when you consider the alternative. –*Maurice Chevalier*
- I look forward to being older, when what you look like becomes less and less an issue and what you are is the point.–*Susan Sarandon*
- There are only three ages for women in Hollywood— Babe, District Attorney, and Driving Miss Daisy. –*Goldie Hawn*
- You know, when I first went into the movies, Lionel Barrymore played my grandfather. Later he played my father, and finally he played my husband. If he had lived, I'm sure I would have played his mother. That's the way it is in Hollywood. The men get younger and the women get older.–*Lillian Gish*
- Old age is like everything else. To make a success of it, you've got to start young.–*Fred Astaire*
- Mistakes are part of the dues that one pays for a full life.–*Sophia Loren*
- What have I done to achieve longevity? Woken up each morning and tried to remember not to wear my hearing aid in the bath.–*Robert Morley*

- I do wish I could tell you my age, but it is impossible. It keeps changing all the time.–*Greer Garson*
- A woman past forty should make up her mind to be young, not her face.–*Billie Burke*
- Age doesn't matter, unless you're a cheese.–*Billie Burke*
- If you survive long enough, you're revered—rather like an old building.–*Katharine Hepburn*
- As you get older, the pickings get slimmer but the people don't.–*Carrie Fisher*
- The best way to get most husbands to do something is to suggest that perhaps they're too old to do it. –*Shirley MacLaine*
- It's not how old you are, but how you are old. –*Marie Dressler*
- If you want a thing done well, get a couple of old broads to do it.–*Bette Davis*
- Love has more depth as you get older.–*Kirk Douglas*
- Memorial services are the cocktail parties of the geriatric set.–*John Gielgud*
- Age does not protect you from love. But love, to some extent, protects you from age.–*Jean Moreau*
- If I had my life to live over again, I'd make the same mistakes, only sooner.–*Tallulah Bankhead*
- Fun is my revenge against mortality.–*Dustin Hoffman*
- Life is a great big canvas. Throw all the paint on it you can.–*Danny Kaye*

41

Writers on Aging

When asked what he wanted to be remembered for when his life was over, best-selling author Leo Buscaglia replied, "I want to be remembered as somebody who lived life fully and with passion. I've been asked to write my epitaph and I have always thought that the perfect one for my tombstone would be, 'Here lies Leo, who died living.'"

It is no surprise that writers, who expostulate about all aspects of life, have lent their insights into the adventure of growing old:

- Nobody loves life like him that's growing old. *–Sophocles*
- To know how to grow old is the masterwork of wisdom, and one of the most difficult chapters in the great art of living.*–Henri-Frédéric Amiel*
- Old wood best to burn, old wine to drink, old friends to trust, and old authors to read.*–Francis Bacon*
- What time hath scanted men in hair, he hath given them in wit.*–William Shakespeare*
- Whenever a man's friends begin to compliment him about looking young, he may be sure they think he is growing old.*–Washington Irving*
- To be seventy years young is sometimes far more cheerful and hopeful than to be forty years old. *–Oliver Wendell Holmes*

- One does not get better but different and older and that is always a pleasure.–*Gertrude Stein*

- To keep the heart unwrinkled, to be hopeful, kindly, cheerful, and reverent–that is to triumph over old age. –*Thomas Bailey Aldrich*

- True terror is to wake up one morning and discover that your high school class is running the country. –*Kurt Vonnegut*

- I have often thought what a melancholy world this would be without children, and what an inhumane world without the aged.–*Samuel Taylor Coleridge*

- What is youth, except a man or a woman before it is ready or fit to be seen?–*Evelyn Waugh*

- Father Time is not always a hard parent, and, though he tarries for none of his children, often lays his hand lightly upon those who have used him well; making them old men and women inexorably enough, but leaving their hearts and spirits young and in full vigor. With such people the gray head is but the impression of the old fellow's hand in giving them his blessing, and every wrinkle but a notch in the quiet calendar of a well-spent life.–*Charles Dickens*

- When grace is joined with wrinkles, it is adorable. There is an unspeakable dawn in happy old age. –*Victor Hugo*

- Old age has its pleasures, which, though different, are not less than the pleasures of youth. –*W. Somerset Maugham*

- To grow old is to pass from passion to compassion. –*Albert Camus*

- It's never too late to be what you might have been. –*George Eliot*

- The years seem to rush by now, and I think of death as a fast-approaching end of a journey. All the more reason for loving as well as working while it is day. *–George Eliot (in the last year of her life)*

- I am in the prime of senility.*–Joel Chandler Harris*
- Someday you will be old enough to start reading fairy tales again.*–C. S. Lewis*
- If you wait, all that happens is that you get older. *–Larry McMurtry*
- No matter how old a mother is, she watches her middle-aged children for signs of improvement. *–Florida Scott-Maxwell*
- Growing old is no more than a bad habit which a busy man has no time to form.*–André Maurois*
- There is no shortage of good days. It is good lives that are hard to come by. A life of good days lived in the senses is not enough. The life of sensation is a life of greed; it requires more and more. The life of the spirit requires less and less; time is ample and its passage sweet.*–Annie Dillard*

Silver Quotations

- We ought not to heap reproaches on old age, seeing that we all hope to reach it.–*Bion*
- Many men die at twenty-five and aren't buried until they are seventy-five.–*Benjamin Franklin*
- Anyone who stops learning is old, whether at twenty or eighty. Anyone who keeps learning stays young. The greatest thing in life is to keep your mind young. –*Henry Ford*
- Those docs, they always ask you how you live so long. I tell 'em: "If I'd known I was going to live so long, I'd have taken better care of myself."–*Eubie Blake*
- Live a good, honorable life. Then, when you get older and think back, you'll be able to enjoy it a second time.–*The Dalai Lama*
- I'm not interested in age. People who tell me their age are silly. You're as old as you feel.–*Elizabeth Arden*
- I refuse to admit that I am more than fifty-two, even if that does make my sons illegitimate.–*Nancy Astor*
- When I was young, I used to have successes with women because I was young. Now I have successes with women because I am old. Middle age was the hard part.–*Arthur Rubinstein*
- Only people who die very young learn all they really need to learn in kindergarten.–*Wendy Kaminer*

CHAPTER 42

- Youth would be an ideal state—if it came a little later in life.–*Lord Asquith*
- I don't care how long I live; I just want to be LIVING while I am living!–*Jack LaLanne*
- The question is not whether we will die, but how we will live.–*Joan Borysenko*
- Age must give way to youth, no doubt. But not yet, not yet.–*Mason Cooley*
- I attribute my longevity to red meat and gin.–*Julia Child*
- Some people, no matter how old they get, never lose their beauty. They merely move it from their faces into their hearts.–*Martin Buxbaum*
- Everyone is the age of their heart.
  –*Guatemalan proverb*
- The key to successful aging is to pay as little attention to it as possible.–*Judith Regan*
- Never use the passing years as an excuse for old age.
  –*Robert Brault*
- You're only as young as the last time you changed your mind.–*Timothy Leary*
- We are only young once. That is all society can stand.
  –*Bob Bowen*
- Getting old is a funny thing. The older you get, the older you want to get.–*Keith Richards*
- At twenty, a man is full of fight and hope. He wants to reform the world. When he is seventy, he still wants to reform the world, but he knows he can't.
  –*Clarence Darrow*
- God planned the strength and beauty of youth to be physical. But the strength and beauty of age is spiritual. We gradually lose the strength and beauty that is temporary so that we'll be sure to concentrate on the strength and beauty that is forever.–*Robert McQuilkin*

• I feel so sorry for folks who don't like to grow old. I revel in my years. They enrich me. I would not exchange the abiding rest of soul; the measure of wisdom I have gained from the sweet and bitter and perplexing experiences of life; nor the confirmed faith I now have in the love of God for all the bright and uncertain hopes and tumultuous joys of youth. Indeed, I would not! These are the best years of my life. The way grows brighter; the birds sing sweeter; the winds blow softer; the sun shines more radiantly than ever before. I suppose "my outward man" is perishing, but "my inward man" is being joyously renewed day by day.–*Henry Durbanville*